Better Homes and Gardens®

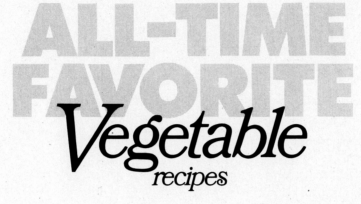

ALL-TIME FAVORITE

Vegetable recipes

On the cover: Garden-fresh peas are a hit any time, but particularly when you serve them in one of these favorite recipes— delicately seasoned *Creamed Peas and Onions* or tomato-studded *Pea-Cheese Salad.*

BETTER HOMES AND GARDENS® BOOKS
Editorial Director: Don Dooley
Executive Editor: Gerald Knox
Art Director: Ernest Shelton
Assistant Art Director: Randall Yontz
Production and Copy Editor: David Kirchner
Food Editor: Doris Eby
Senior Associate Food Editor: Nancy Morton
Senior Food Editors: Elizabeth Strait,
   Sharyl Heiken
Associate Food Editors: Flora Szatkowski,
   Sandra Granseth, Diane Nelson
Graphic Designers: Sheryl Veenschoten,
   Faith Berven, Harijs Priekulis

Our seal assures you that every recipe in *All-Time Favorite Vegetable Recipes* is endorsed by the Better Homes and Gardens Test Kitchen. Each recipe is tested for family appeal, practicality, and deliciousness.

Contents

VEGETABLE COOKERY
ARTICHOKES TO ZUCCHINI

Show your family the difference between ordinary and *vibrant* vegetables with the recipes in this book. From dishes you've requested and made popular to some of our own favorites, we've cooked up a collection of specialties to tempt even the reluctant vegetable fan at your table.

Harvest table of vegetable dishes holds (clockwise, beginning top left): *Whipped Parsnips and Sweet Potatoes, Saucy Brussels Sprouts, Oxtail-Leek Stew, Sausage-Stuffed Turban Squash, Squash Soufflé,* and *Zesty Vegetable Salad* (see Index for recipe pages).

Artichokes

Selecting: Although most plentiful during the spring months, Globe artichokes are available year-round. Look for compact green artichokes with tightly closed leaves. You can store them, unwashed, in your refrigerator several days.

Preparing: Wash, trim stems, and remove loose outer leaves. Cut off 1 inch of tops; snip off sharp leaf tips. Brush cut edges with lemon juice.

Cooking: In large covered kettle simmer in boiling salted water till a leaf pulls out easily, 20 to 30 minutes. Drain upside down.

Serving: Offer cooked whole artichokes, hot or cold, with a favorite sauce. To eat, pull off a leaf and dip the base of the leaf in sauce. Draw through teeth, eating only the tender flesh. Discard rest of leaf. Continue till a cone of young leaves appears. Pull away the cone, eating the little bit of soft flesh, then scoop out and discard the fuzzy "choke." Eat the remaining heart with a fork, dipping each piece in sauce.

Jerusalem Artichokes: These tuberous vegetables resemble Globe artichokes in flavor. Serve raw in salads, or baked or boiled as a cooked vegetable.

Artichoke-Crab Entrée

- **4 artichokes**
- **1 tablespoon finely chopped green onion with tops**
- **1 clove garlic, minced**
- **2 small bay leaves, crushed**
- **¼ cup butter *or* margarine**
- **¼ cup all-purpose flour**
  Dash pepper
- **1 12-ounce can clam juice**
- **1 7½-ounce can crab meat, drained, flaked, and cartilage removed**
- **¼ cup grated Parmesan cheese**
- **¼ cup dry white wine**
- **1 1-ounce triangle Gruyère cheese**

Prepare, cook, and drain artichokes as directed above. Cut off and discard remaining top fourth of artichokes, trim stems so artichokes sit flat, and remove center leaves and chokes. Place artichokes in an 8x8x2-inch baking dish.

In medium skillet cook green onion, garlic, and bay leaves in butter or margarine till onion is tender but not brown. Blend in flour and pepper. Add clam juice; cook quickly, stirring constantly, till mixture thickens and bubbles. Stir in crab meat, Parmesan cheese, and dry white wine. Spoon crab mixture into the artichokes. Slice Gruyère cheese into 4 triangles; place 1 triangle atop each artichoke. Pour boiling water into baking dish around artichokes to depth of ½ inch. Cap loosely with foil. Bake at 375° till heated through, 25 to 30 minutes. Makes 4 servings.

Sunburst Artichoke

1 medium artichoke
½ cup mayonnaise *or* salad
dressing
1 teaspoon dry mustard
½ teaspoon Worcestershire sauce
3 hard-cooked eggs

Prepare, cook, and drain artichoke as directed on page 6. Chill thoroughly. Pull off leaves. Combine mayonnaise, mustard, and Worcestershire. Halve hard-cooked eggs crosswise; cut each half into 8 wedges. Dollop about ½ teaspoon mayonnaise mixture at base of each artichoke leaf; place an egg wedge atop mixture on each leaf. Arrange leaves sunburst fashion on a plate. Makes about 48.

Italian-Dipped Artichokes (pictured on page 9)

2 artichokes
1 8-ounce container sour cream
dip with French onion
2 tablespoons finely chopped
green pepper
1 tablespoon snipped parsley
1 teaspoon lemon juice
½ teaspoon dried oregano,
crushed

Prepare, cook, and drain artichokes as directed on page 6. Remove center leaves and chokes. Chill thoroughly.

Meanwhile, combine sour cream dip, green pepper, parsley, lemon juice, oregano, and dash pepper; chill well. Serve sauce with chilled artichokes. Makes 1 cup sauce.

Artichokes Parmesan

8 small artichokes
1 tablespoon sliced green onion
with tops
1 clove garlic, minced
3 tablespoons butter *or*
margarine
1½ cups soft bread crumbs
¼ cup grated Parmesan cheese
2 tablespoons snipped parsley

Prepare artichokes as directed on page 6, trimming stems so they sit flat. Remove center leaves and chokes. Do not cook. Cook onion and garlic in butter till tender. Combine bread crumbs, Parmesan, and parsley. Add onion mixture; mix lightly. Spoon into artichokes. Place stuffed artichokes in large saucepan, making sure artichokes won't tip over. Pour water around artichokes in saucepan to a depth of 1 inch. Bring to boiling; reduce heat. Cover tightly; simmer till artichokes are done, about 30 minutes. Add a little additional water during cooking, if necessary. Makes 8 servings.

Artichokes with Lemon Butter Sauce

Artichokes
¼ cup butter *or* margarine
1 tablespoon snipped parsley
1 tablespoon lemon juice

Prepare, cook, and drain artichokes as directed on page 6. Meanwhile, melt butter or margarine; stir in snipped parsley, lemon juice, and dash pepper. Serve butter sauce with cooked artichokes. Makes ⅓ cup sauce.

Jerusalem Artichokes with Parslied Cream Sauce

1 pound Jerusalem artichokes
2 tablespoons butter
2 tablespoons all-purpose flour
½ teaspoon salt
Dash white pepper
1 cup light cream *or* milk
¼ cup finely snipped parsley

Wash and peel Jerusalem artichokes; slice. In covered pan cook in a small amount of boiling salted water till tender, 10 to 15 minutes. Drain well. Melt butter in a saucepan; blend in flour, salt, and white pepper. Add cream or milk all at once. Cook and stir till thickened and bubbly. Remove from heat. Stir in snipped parsley. Serve sauce over cooked Jerusalem artichokes. Makes 4 to 6 servings.

Asparagus

Selecting: Fresh asparagus is in season mid-February through June. Choose firm, straight stalks with compact, closed tips. Asparagus with wilted stalks or loose tips is apt to be tough and stringy. Wrap stem ends in moist paper toweling before refrigerating in a plastic bag. Asparagus keeps one or two days.

Preparing: Wash and scrape off scales. Break off woody bases at point where spears snap easily.

Cooking: Place whole spears in a skillet or saucepan in a small amount of boiling salted water. To avoid overcooking tips, prop up out of water with crumpled foil. Or, fasten whole spears in a bundle and stand upright in a deep kettle, letting tips extend 2 to 3 inches above boiling salted water. Cover pan and cook till spears are crisp-tender, 10 to 15 minutes. Cook cut-up asparagus for 8 to 10 minutes.

Tip: Make a foil strainer to remove cooked asparagus easily without breaking the tips. Tear off foil strip long enough to cover bottom, sides, and edges of a saucepan. Fold to a 4-inch width. Cook asparagus spears atop foil, then remove by lifting ends of foil strip.

Asparagus Omelet Tarragon

½ pound asparagus, bias-sliced
  into 1-inch pieces
6 eggs
2 tablespoons water
¼ teaspoon salt
  Dash pepper
2 tablespoons butter *or*
  margarine
  Golden Tarragon Sauce

Cook cut-up fresh asparagus as directed above. Drain well; keep warm. Beat eggs, water, salt, and pepper with fork till blended but not frothy. In 10-inch skillet or omelet pan heat butter or margarine till it sizzles and browns slightly. Tilt pan to grease sides. Add egg mixture and cook slowly. Run spatula around edge, lifting egg to allow uncooked portion to flow underneath. Spoon asparagus across center of omelet; top with ½ cup Golden Tarragon Sauce. Tilt pan to fold omelet and roll onto hot platter. Serve with remaining Golden Tarragon Sauce. Makes 4 servings.

Golden Tarragon Sauce: In small saucepan cook ¼ cup sliced green onion with tops in 1 tablespoon butter till tender. Stir in 3 tablespoons dry white wine and 1 tablespoon white wine vinegar. Simmer till liquid is reduced by half, 3 to 5 minutes. In another saucepan melt 1 tablespoon butter; blend in 4 teaspoons all-purpose flour. Add 1¼ cups milk. Cook, stirring constantly, till thickened and bubbly. Remove from heat; stir in ¼ teaspoon salt and ¼ teaspoon dried tarragon, crushed. Return to low heat and slowly stir in onion mixture. Heat through, but *do not boil.*

Start with spring vegetables to create *Italian-Dipped Artichokes* (see page 7), *Asparagus with Orange Hollandaise Sauce* (see page 10), and elegant *Asparagus Omelet Tarragon.*

Asparagus Vinaigrette

¾ **pound asparagus *or***
   1 8-ounce package frozen
   asparagus spears
½ **cup salad oil**
2 **tablespoons vinegar**
2 **tablespoons lemon juice**
2 **teaspoons sugar**
½ **teaspoon salt**
½ **teaspoon paprika**
½ **teaspoon dry mustard**
   Dash cayenne
2 **tablespoons finely chopped**
   pimiento-stuffed green
   olives
1 **hard-cooked egg, finely**
   chopped
2 **small tomatoes, chilled**
   Lettuce leaves

Cook the fresh asparagus spears as directed on page 8. (Or, cook frozen asparagus according to package directions.) Drain. In screw-top jar combine salad oil, vinegar, lemon juice, sugar, salt, paprika, dry mustard, and cayenne. Add the pimiento-stuffed olives and chopped hard-cooked egg; cover and shake well. Arrange asparagus in a shallow dish; top with vinegar mixture. Cover and refrigerate for several hours or overnight, spooning vinegar mixture over asparagus occasionally.

To serve, drain asparagus, reserving vinegar mixture. Slice tomatoes. On each of 4 salad plates, arrange a few asparagus spears atop lettuce. Top each salad with a few tomato slices. Spoon a little of the reserved vinegar mixture over each salad. Makes 4 servings.

Asparagus with Orange Hollandaise Sauce (pictured on page 9)

1 pound asparagus
¼ cup butter *or* margarine, softened
2 egg yolks
¼ teaspoon finely shredded
　　orange peel
1 teaspoon orange juice
　Dash salt
　Dash white pepper
¼ cup dairy sour cream

Cook fresh asparagus as directed on page 8. Drain well. Meanwhile, divide butter into 3 portions. In small heavy saucepan combine egg yolks and 1 portion of the butter. Cook and stir over *low* heat till butter melts. Add another portion of the butter and continue stirring. As mixture thickens and butter melts, add remaining butter, stirring constantly. When butter is melted, remove from heat. Stir in orange peel, orange juice, salt, and white pepper. Return to *low* heat. Cook and stir till thickened, 2 to 3 minutes. Remove from heat at once. Blend hot mixture into sour cream. Spoon over asparagus. Garnish with more finely shredded orange peel, if desired. Makes 4 or 5 servings.

Sesame Asparagus

2 8-ounce packages frozen cut
　　asparagus
1 2½-ounce jar sliced mushrooms,
　　drained
2 tablespoons butter *or*
　　margarine
1 teaspoon lemon juice
1 teaspoon sesame seed, toasted

Cook frozen asparagus according to package directions. Drain well. Season to taste with salt and pepper. Gently stir in mushrooms, butter, and lemon juice. Cook until heated through. Turn mixture into serving bowl; sprinkle with sesame seed. Makes 6 servings.

Microwave cooking directions: Place frozen asparagus in 1½-quart nonmetal casserole. Cook, covered, in countertop microwave oven till tender, about 10 minutes, stirring twice. Drain well. Season. Gently stir in mushrooms, butter, and lemon juice. Micro-cook, covered, till heated through, about 2 minutes, stirring once. Serve as above.

Stir-Fry Beef with Asparagus

1 pound beef flank steak,
　　partially frozen
2 tablespoons soy sauce
1 tablespoon cooking oil
1 tablespoon cornstarch
12 asparagus spears
3 tablespoons cooking oil
1 teaspoon sugar
2 tablespoons dry sherry
2 tablespoons chicken broth

Using a sharp knife, cut flank steak across grain into very thin slices. Blend soy sauce and the 1 tablespoon oil into the cornstarch; pour over beef slices, stirring to coat. Bias-slice asparagus into 1-inch pieces. Drop asparagus into a pan of boiling water. Simmer for 1 to 2 minutes; drain. In wok or skillet heat the 3 tablespoons oil till sizzling. Sprinkle sugar over oil. Add beef; cook and stir for 1 minute. Add asparagus; cook and stir 1 minute longer. Add sherry and chicken broth; cook ½ minute longer. Arrange meat and asparagus on serving platter. Serve with hot cooked rice, if desired. Serves 4.

Chilled Asparagus Soup

¾ pound asparagus, cut up, *or*
　　1 8-ounce package frozen
　　cut asparagus
1 thin slice onion
½ cup boiling water
1 cup milk
½ cup light cream
½ teaspoon salt
　Dash pepper

In covered pan cook fresh or frozen asparagus and the onion slice in the boiling water till crisp-tender; do not drain. Cool slightly. In blender container combine the undrained asparagus and onion, milk, light cream, salt, and pepper. Cover and blend until smooth, 15 to 20 seconds. Chill for 3 to 4 hours (chill in blender container, if desired). Stir or blend before serving. Makes 4 to 6 servings.

Beans

Selecting: Green and wax beans are grown for the tender, fleshy pod. Choose long, straight pods that snap crisply when bent. Lima and fava beans are usually cultivated for the seed. Select dark green, crisp, full pods (fava pods are lima-like in shape, but thicker and slightly larger). The shelled beans should be plump with a tender green or greenish-white skin. You can store unshelled fresh beans in the refrigerator for a few days. Dry beans are available in numerous varieties. When selecting, discard beans that are wrinkled or discolored. Store in tightly covered container in cool, dry place.

Preparing: Wash green and wax beans; remove ends and strings. Leave whole, or cut in 1-inch pieces. For French-style, slice diagonally end to end. Shell limas or favas and wash. Rinse dry beans; place in heavy saucepan or kettle with about 3 times as much water as beans. Cover pan; soak overnight. (Or, bring to boiling; simmer for 2 minutes. Remove from heat. Cover pan; soak at least 1 hour.) Do not drain.

Cooking: In covered pan cook whole or cut fresh beans in small amount of boiling salted water till crisp-tender, 20 to 30 minutes. Cook French-style beans 10 to 12 minutes. Cover and simmer dry beans till tender.

Green Beans Supreme

1 pound green beans *or*
  2 9-ounce packages frozen French-style green beans
1 small onion, sliced
1 tablespoon snipped parsley
3 tablespoons butter
2 tablespoons all-purpose flour
½ teaspoon finely shredded lemon peel
½ cup milk
1 cup dairy sour cream
½ cup shredded American cheese
¼ cup fine dry bread crumbs

Cut fresh beans French-style and cook as directed above. (Or, cook frozen beans according to package directions.) Drain. Cook onion and parsley in *2 tablespoons* of the butter till onion is tender. Blend in flour, lemon peel, ½ teaspoon salt, and dash pepper. Add milk; cook and stir till thickened and bubbly. Stir in sour cream and cooked beans; heat till just bubbly. Spoon into 1-quart casserole. Sprinkle with cheese. Melt the remaining 1 tablespoon butter; toss with bread crumbs and sprinkle atop beans. Broil 4 to 5 inches from heat till cheese melts and crumbs brown, 1 to 2 minutes. Makes 8 servings.

Creamy Lima Beans

1 pound lima beans, shelled
(2 cups), *or* 1 10-ounce
package frozen lima beans
2 tablespoons sliced green
onion with tops
1 tablespoon butter *or* margarine
1 tablespoon all-purpose flour
½ cup milk
2 tablespoons brown sugar
½ cup dairy sour cream

Cook fresh lima beans as directed on page 11. (Or, cook frozen limas according to package directions.) Drain well. In medium saucepan cook green onion in butter or margarine till tender but not brown. Blend in flour, ¼ teaspoon salt, and dash pepper. Add milk and brown sugar. Cook, stirring constantly, till thickened and bubbly. Stir sour cream and drained cooked limas into sauce mixture. Heat through, but *do not boil*. Makes 4 servings.

Mustard Beans

1 pound wax beans *or* 1 15½-ounce
can whole wax beans, drained
½ cup sugar
½ cup vinegar
¼ cup prepared mustard
2 tablespoons finely chopped
onion
¼ teaspoon salt

Cook the whole fresh wax beans as directed on page 11. Drain. In saucepan combine sugar, vinegar, mustard, onion, salt, and ⅓ cup water. Bring mixture to boiling, stirring till sugar dissolves. Add drained cooked fresh beans or the drained canned beans. Simmer, uncovered, for 5 minutes; cool. Cover and refrigerate several hours or overnight, stirring occasionally. Makes 2 cups relish.

Two-Bean Fritters

1 cup green beans cut
in ½-inch pieces
1 cup wax beans cut
in ½-inch pieces
1½ cups all-purpose flour
1 tablespoon baking powder
1 beaten egg
1 cup milk
Fat for deep-fat frying

Cook green and wax beans as directed on page 11. Drain well. Stir together flour, baking powder, and ¾ teaspoon salt. Combine egg, milk, and cooked beans. Add to dry ingredients, mixing just till moistened. Drop batter by tablespoonfuls into deep hot fat (375°). Fry, several at a time, till golden brown, 3 to 4 minutes. Drain on paper toweling. Makes about 24 vegetable fritters.

Baked Bean Cassoulet

1 pound dry navy beans (2⅓ cups)
1 cup chopped celery
1 cup chopped carrot
2 teaspoons instant beef
bouillon granules
1 teaspoon salt
1 2½- to 3-pound ready-to-cook
broiler-fryer chicken with
giblets, cut up
½ pound bulk pork sausage
1 cup chopped onion
1½ cups tomato juice
1 tablespoon Worcestershire
sauce
½ teaspoon paprika

Soak dry beans, using 8 cups water, as directed on page 11. Stir in celery, carrot, bouillon granules, and salt. Add giblets from chicken (refrigerate remaining chicken). Bring to boil; reduce heat. Cover; simmer 1 hour. Shape sausage into small balls; brown in large skillet. Remove sausage; set aside. Reserve drippings in skillet. Season chicken generously with salt and pepper; brown in reserved drippings. Remove chicken; set aside. In same skillet cook onion till tender. Stir in tomato juice and Worcestershire.

Drain bean mixture, reserving liquid. Combine bean mixture, sausage, and tomato mixture. Turn into 6-quart Dutch oven. Top with chicken; add 1½ cups of the reserved liquid. Sprinkle with paprika. Cover; bake at 325° for 1 hour, adding more bean liquid for moistness, if needed. Makes 8 servings.

You'll find our adaptation of a classic French specialty, *Baked Bean Cassoulet*, as tasty as the original. Chicken pieces and sausage balls complement the seasoned navy beans.

New England Baked Beans

1 **pound dry navy beans (2⅓ cups)**
8 **cups water**
½ **teaspoon salt**
½ **cup light molasses**
¼ **cup packed brown sugar**
1 **teaspoon dry mustard**
½ **teaspoon salt**
⅛ **teaspoon pepper**
4 **ounces salt pork, cut in small pieces (1 cup)**
1 **large onion, chopped**

Soak dry navy beans, using 8 cups water, as directed on page 11. Add the ½ teaspoon salt. Bring to boiling; reduce heat. Cover and simmer till beans are tender, about 1 hour. Drain, reserving bean liquid.

Combine molasses, brown sugar, mustard, the remaining ½ teaspoon salt, and pepper. Stir in 2 cups of the reserved bean liquid. In 2-quart bean pot or casserole combine cooked beans, salt pork, onion, and molasses mixture. Cover and bake at 300° for 3½ hours. Stir beans occasionally. Stir in a little of the reserved bean liquid or water for moistness, if necessary. Makes 6 to 8 servings.

Crockery cooker directions: Rinse beans. In large heavy saucepan combine beans, water, and ½ teaspoon salt. Bring mixture to boiling; reduce heat. Cover and simmer for 1½ hours. Pour into a bowl. Cover and refrigerate overnight. Drain beans, reserving 1 cup liquid.

Place beans in an electric slow crockery cooker. Combine molasses, brown sugar, mustard, ½ teaspoon salt, pepper, and reserved liquid. Add to beans with salt pork and onion; mix well. Cover and cook on low-heat setting for 12 to 14 hours. Stir before serving.

Green Beans Amandine

1 **pound green beans**
2 **tablespoons slivered almonds**
2 **tablespoons butter**
1 **teaspoon lemon juice**

Cut green beans French-style and cook as directed on page 11. Drain. Meanwhile, cook slivered almonds in butter over low heat, stirring occasionally, till golden. Remove from heat; add lemon juice. Pour over beans. Makes 4 servings.

Green Bean Bake with Onion

2 **9-ounce packages frozen *or* 2 16-ounce cans French-style green beans**
1 **10¾-ounce can condensed cream of mushroom soup**
2 **tablespoons chopped pimiento**
1 **teaspoon lemon juice**
½ **of a 3-ounce can French-fried onions**

Cook frozen beans according to package directions; drain. (Or, drain canned beans.) Combine the cooked frozen or the canned beans, mushroom soup, pimiento, and lemon juice. Turn mixture into a 1-quart casserole. Bake, uncovered, at 350° for 35 minutes. Sprinkle with French-fried onions. Continue baking, uncovered, till onions are heated through, about 5 minutes longer. Makes 6 servings.

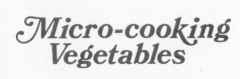
Micro-cooking Vegetables

Microwave cooking is an excellent way to prepare colorful, flavorful, and nutritious vegetables. The countertop microwave oven will also save you time, as you'll see in selected recipes throughout the book.

When preparing vegetables, micro-cook them just till almost done; they'll finish cooking with stored heat. Season with salt after cooking to avoid drying out the vegetables. For basic vegetable cookery, follow your owner's manual.

Spanish String Beans

1 pound green beans, cut in
   1-inch pieces (3 cups)
½ cup chopped green pepper
¼ cup chopped onion
1 tablespoon olive oil *or*
   cooking oil
2 medium tomatoes, peeled and
   chopped
1 teaspoon salt
½ teaspoon dried basil, crushed
¼ teaspoon dried rosemary,
   crushed

Cook fresh cut-up green beans as directed on page 11; drain. Meanwhile, cook chopped green pepper and onion in hot olive oil or cooking oil till tender but not brown. Add chopped tomatoes, salt, basil, rosemary, and ⅛ teaspoon pepper. Stir in cooked green beans; heat through. Season to taste with salt and pepper. Makes 8 servings.

Marinated Three-Bean Salad

1 8½-ounce can lima beans
1 8-ounce can cut green beans
1 8-ounce can red kidney beans
1 medium sweet onion, sliced and
   separated into rings
½ cup chopped green pepper
⅔ cup vinegar
½ cup salad oil
¼ cup sugar
1 teaspoon celery seed

Drain canned beans. In large bowl combine lima beans, green beans, red kidney beans, onion rings, and green pepper. In a screw-top jar combine vinegar, salad oil, sugar, and celery seed; cover and shake well. Pour vinegar mixture over vegetables and stir lightly. Cover and refrigerate for 8 hours or overnight, stirring occasionally. Drain before serving. Makes 8 servings.

Easy Baked Beans

4 slices bacon
½ cup chopped onion
2 16-ounce cans pork and beans
   in tomato sauce
2 tablespoons brown sugar
2 tablespoons catsup
1 tablespoon Worcestershire
   sauce
1 tablespoon prepared mustard

Cook bacon till crisp. Remove bacon, reserving about 3 tablespoons drippings in skillet. Crumble bacon and set aside. Cook onion in reserved drippings till tender. Stir in pork and beans, brown sugar, catsup, Worcestershire, and mustard. Turn into 1½-quart casserole. Bake, uncovered, at 350° for 1½ to 1¾ hours. Stir; top with bacon. Let stand a few minutes before serving. Makes 6 servings.

Mexican Lima Beans

1 pound large dry lima beans
   (2½ cups)
1 15-ounce can tomato sauce
1 medium onion, sliced
⅓ cup chili sauce
¼ cup chopped green pepper
1 teaspoon salt
1 teaspoon chili powder
1 cup dairy sour cream
¼ cup shredded American cheese
½ cup crushed corn chips

Soak dry lima beans, using 8 cups water, as directed on page 11. Bring mixture to boiling; reduce heat. Cover and simmer till lima beans are just tender, 30 to 40 minutes. Drain, reserving 1 cup of the bean liquid.
   In 2-quart casserole combine beans, reserved liquid, tomato sauce, onion, chili sauce, green pepper, salt, and chili powder. Cover; bake at 300° for 2½ hours. Spread sour cream over top; sprinkle with cheese. Sprinkle chips around edge. Bake for 5 minutes more. Makes 8 servings.

Beets

Selecting: Markets supply fresh garden beets year-round. Choose round, small-to-medium beets with a smooth, firm, deep red flesh and a slender tap root. Large beets may be woody. Spring beets are often sold in bunches with the tender, young tops still intact (to allow for weight of tops, buy about ½ pound more for each pound of beets needed). If fresh and reasonably unblemished, the tops make good eating (see Greens). You can store fresh beets with tops in the refrigerator crisper for a few days. Late-crop beets are usually sold without tops and can be stored for longer periods.

Preparing: Cut off all but 1 inch of stems and roots; wash. Leave whole beets unpeeled. Or, peel beets and slice, cube, or shred.

Cooking: In covered pan cook whole beets in boiling salted water till tender, 35 to 50 minutes. Cool slightly and slip off skins. Cook sliced or cubed beets in small amount of water for 15 to 20 minutes; shredded beets about 10 minutes.

Serving: Enjoy beets tossed with a little melted butter or heavy cream and seasoned with herbs.

Borscht with Mushroom Dumplings

1 ounce *dried* mushrooms (¾ cup)
3½ cups boiling water
2 pounds beets, peeled,
    thinly sliced, and quartered
4 cups water
1 cup chopped carrot
1 cup chopped celery
½ cup chopped onion
2 bay leaves
1 teaspoon salt
2 tablespoons vinegar
1 teaspoon sugar
1 teaspoon salt
⅛ teaspoon pepper
    Mushroom Dumplings

Combine mushrooms with boiling water. Let soak 2 hours at room temperature. Simmer, uncovered, till tender, 7 to 10 minutes. Drain; reserve liquid. Set mushrooms aside.

In large saucepan combine next 7 ingredients. Cover and cook till vegetables are tender, 40 to 45 minutes. Remove bay leaves. Stir in reserved mushroom liquid, vinegar, sugar, the 1 teaspoon salt, and pepper. Bring to boil. Ladle into bowls; add Mushroom Dumplings to each serving. Serves 10.

Mushroom Dumplings: Mix 1 cup all-purpose flour, 1 beaten egg, 2 to 3 tablespoons water, and ¼ teaspoon salt. Knead on floured surface till smooth and elastic. Cover; let stand 10 minutes. Cook 2 tablespoons chopped onion in 1 tablespoon butter. Chop reserved mushrooms; add to onion mixture with 1 tablespoon fine dry bread crumbs, 1 egg white, ¼ teaspoon salt, and dash pepper. Divide dough in half. Roll each half ⅛ inch thick; cut in 1½-inch squares. Top each with ½ teaspoon mushroom mixture; fold into triangle. Seal. Cook in large amount boiling salted water 5 minutes.

When it's too hot to cook, toss together this cool and colorful *Beet Supper Salad.*
Sweet and juicy red beets and tender leaf lettuce contribute fresh-from-the-garden flavor.

Beet Supper Salad

1 **pound beets**
1 **small clove garlic, halved**
6 **cups leaf lettuce**
¼ **cup sliced green onion with tops**
1 **6½- *or* 7-ounce can tuna, chilled and well drained**
½ **cup sliced celery**
2 **hard-cooked eggs, chopped**
½ **cup mayonnaise *or* salad dressing**
½ **teaspoon salt**
Dash pepper
Sliced green onion with tops (optional)

Cook fresh whole beets as directed on page 16. Drain, peel, and slice cooked beets. Chill. Just before serving, rub a salad bowl with halved garlic. Combine leaf lettuce and the ¼ cup green onion in salad bowl. Arrange beets, tuna, celery, and hard-cooked eggs atop. Combine mayonnaise or salad dressing, salt, and pepper; dollop in center of salad. Garnish with additional sliced green onion, if desired. To serve, gently toss mayonnaise mixture with the salad ingredients. Makes 6 to 8 servings.

Harvard Beets

1 8¼-ounce can sliced beets
1 tablespoon sugar
1 teaspoon cornstarch
⅛ teaspoon salt
2 tablespoons vinegar
1 tablespoon butter *or* margarine

Drain beets, reserving ¼ cup liquid. In saucepan combine sugar, cornstarch, and salt. Stir in reserved beet liquid, the vinegar, and butter. Cook, stirring constantly, till mixture is thickened and bubbly. Stir in beets. Cook until heated through. Makes 2 servings.

Microwave cooking directions: Drain beets; reserve ¼ cup liquid. In a 2-cup glass measure combine sugar, cornstarch, and salt. Stir in reserved liquid, vinegar, and butter. Cook, uncovered, in countertop microwave oven till thick and bubbly, about 1 minute; stir every 15 seconds. Stir in beets. Micro-cook, covered, till hot, about 2 minutes.

Beet and Pineapple Mold

1 16-ounce can diced *or*
   shoestring beets
1 8¼-ounce can crushed pineapple
1 6-ounce package lemon-flavored
   gelatin
2 cups boiling water
3 tablespoons lemon juice
   Dash salt
½ cup chopped celery

Drain beets and pineapple, reserving liquids. Combine liquids and add water to make 1½ cups. Dissolve gelatin in boiling water; stir in reserved liquid mixture, lemon juice, and salt. Chill till partially set. Fold in drained beets, pineapple, and chopped celery. Pour gelatin mixture into a 6½-cup mold. Chill till firm. Makes 8 to 10 servings.

Beets with Sour Cream

1 pound beets
½ cup dairy sour cream
2 tablespoons milk
1 tablespoon sliced green onion
   with tops
1 tablespoon vinegar
1 teaspoon sugar
¼ teaspoon salt
   Dash cayenne

Peel and slice beets; halve slices. Cook beets as directed on page 16. Drain. Meanwhile, in small saucepan combine sour cream, milk, green onion, vinegar, sugar, salt, and cayenne. Heat through over low heat, but *do not boil*. Turn beets into serving dish; spoon sour cream mixture atop. Stir to combine, if desired. Makes 4 servings.

Beet-Apple Relish

3 pounds beets, cooked,
   peeled, and cut up (6 cups)
6 large apples, peeled, cored,
   and quartered
2 large onions, cut up
4 inches stick cinnamon, broken
1½ cups sugar
1½ cups vinegar
½ cup water
1 tablespoon salt

Put beets, apples, and onions through a food grinder, using coarse blade. In large kettle or Dutch oven combine ground mixture, cinnamon, sugar, vinegar, water, and salt. Bring to boiling; reduce heat. Cover and simmer 20 minutes, stirring often. Remove cinnamon. Ladle hot relish into hot, clean half-pint jars, leaving ½-inch headspace.

Prepare lids according to manufacturer's directions. Wipe jar rim. Adjust lid on jar. Process jars in boiling water bath for 15 minutes. (Start timing when water returns to boiling.) Makes 11 half-pints.

Broccoli

Selecting: Broccoli grows year-round, but the supply is smallest during the hot summer months. Look for firm, tender stalks bearing small, crisp leaves. The dark green or purplish-green buds should be tightly closed, showing no signs of flowering. You can store broccoli in the refrigerator crisper in a plastic bag for a few days.

Preparing: Wash broccoli; remove the outer leaves and tough part of stalks. Cut broccoli stalks lengthwise into uniform spears, following the branching lines.

Cooking: In covered pan cook spears in 1 inch of boiling salted water till crisp-tender, 10 to 15 minutes. For cut-up broccoli, cut off the buds and set aside. Cut the remaining part of spears into 1-inch pieces; in covered pan cook in boiling salted water 5 to 8 minutes. Add the reserved broccoli buds and cook about 5 minutes longer.

Serving: A variety of sauces complements the flavor of cooked broccoli. Try hollandaise, cheese, mayonnaise, or mustard sauce over individual servings.

Broccoli-Egg Bake

1 pound broccoli *or* 2 10-ounce packages frozen broccoli spears
6 hard-cooked eggs
½ cup finely chopped fully cooked ham
2 tablespoons butter, softened
1 tablespoon finely chopped onion
½ teaspoon Worcestershire sauce
¼ teaspoon dry mustard
¼ cup butter *or* margarine
¼ cup all-purpose flour
¼ teaspoon salt
2½ cups milk
1 cup shredded sharp American cheese (4 ounces)
1½ cups soft bread crumbs
¼ cup butter, melted

Cut fresh broccoli stalks into spears and cook as directed above. (Or, cook frozen broccoli according to package directions.) Drain. Halve the hard-cooked eggs. Remove egg yolks; set egg whites aside. Mash egg yolks; stir in chopped ham, the 2 tablespoons softened butter, onion, Worcestershire sauce, and dry mustard. Fill egg whites with yolk mixture. Arrange cooked broccoli in a 12x7½x2-inch baking dish; top with the filled eggs.

In saucepan melt ¼ cup butter. Blend in flour and salt. Stir in milk; cook quickly, stirring constantly, till mixture is thickened and bubbly. Add shredded American cheese; stir till melted. Pour sauce mixture over broccoli and eggs. Toss bread crumbs with ¼ cup melted butter; sprinkle over casserole. Bake at 350° till heated through, about 25 minutes. Makes 6 servings.

Whether your meal is simple or formal, *Broccoli-Onion Deluxe* is an excellent choice
for entertaining. This colorful casserole features two popular vegetables in a creamy sauce.

Broccoli-Onion Deluxe

1 pound broccoli *or* 2 10-ounce
    packages frozen cut broccoli
2 cups frozen small whole onions
    or 3 medium onions,
    quartered
¼ cup butter *or* margarine
2 tablespoons all-purpose flour
¼ teaspoon salt
1 cup milk
1 3-ounce package cream cheese
½ cup shredded sharp American
    cheese (2 ounces)
1 cup soft bread crumbs

Cut up fresh broccoli and cook as directed on page 19. (Or, cook frozen broccoli according to package directions.) Drain. Cook frozen or fresh onions in boiling salted water till tender. Drain. In saucepan melt *half* of the butter or margarine. Blend in flour, salt, and dash pepper. Add milk. Cook, stirring constantly, till thickened and bubbly. Reduce heat; blend in cream cheese till smooth.

Place vegetables in a 1½-quart casserole. Pour sauce mixture over and mix lightly. Top with American cheese. Melt the remaining butter; toss with bread crumbs. Sprinkle atop casserole. Bake at 350° till heated through, 40 to 45 minutes. Makes 6 servings.

Broccoli Soufflé

2 cups chopped broccoli *or*
    1 10-ounce package frozen
    chopped broccoli
2 tablespoons butter *or*
    margarine
2 tablespoons all-purpose flour
½ teaspoon salt
½ cup milk
4 egg yolks
¼ cup grated Parmesan cheese
4 egg whites

In covered pan cook fresh chopped broccoli in boiling salted water 8 to 10 minutes. (Or, cook frozen broccoli according to package directions.) Drain well. Chop any large pieces. Melt butter; blend in flour and salt. Add milk. Cook and stir till bubbly; remove from heat. Beat egg yolks till thick and lemon-colored. Slowly stir half of hot mixture into yolks; return to hot mixture. Stir rapidly. Stir in cheese and broccoli. Beat egg whites till stiff peaks form; fold into broccoli mixture. Turn into *ungreased* 1-quart soufflé dish. Bake at 350° till knife inserted off-center comes out clean, 35 to 40 minutes. Serve at once. Serves 4.

Lemon Broccoli

1½ pounds broccoli *or* 3 10-ounce
    packages frozen broccoli spears
½ cup chopped green onion
    with tops
½ cup chopped celery
6 tablespoons butter
2 tablespoons lemon juice
½ teaspoon finely shredded lemon
    peel

Cut fresh broccoli stalks into spears and cook as directed on page 19. (Or, cook frozen broccoli spears according to package directions.) Drain well. In small saucepan cook green onion and celery in butter till tender but not brown. Stir in lemon juice; heat through. To serve, layer broccoli and butter mixture in a serving dish. Sprinkle with shredded lemon peel. Makes 8 servings.

Curried Broccoli Salad

½ pound broccoli
1 cup dairy sour cream
¼ cup milk
½ teaspoon curry powder
¼ teaspoon seasoned salt
¼ teaspoon dry mustard
3 medium tomatoes, cut in wedges
    Lettuce

Remove the broccoli buds; use stalks another time. In covered pan cook broccoli buds in boiling salted water till crisp-tender, about 5 minutes. Drain well. Cool.

Combine sour cream, milk, curry powder, seasoned salt, dry mustard, and dash pepper. Pour over broccoli buds, stirring to coat. Cover and chill for 2 to 3 hours. To serve, arrange broccoli buds and tomato wedges on a bed of lettuce. Makes 5 or 6 servings.

Brussels Sprouts

Selecting: These dense, compact buds resembling miniature cabbages receive their name from their area of origin, the Belgian city of Brussels. They're at their best between October and March. Select small-to-medium sprouts of a vivid green color with tight-fitting outer leaves. Store, unwashed, in a plastic bag in the refrigerator crisper. Sprouts keep for one or two days.

Preparing: Trim stems slightly, remove wilted or discolored leaves, and wash. Cut any large sprouts in half lengthwise.

Cooking: In covered pan cook sprouts in small amount boiling salted water till crisp-tender, 10 to 15 minutes.

Serving: An especially popular way to serve this nutty-flavored winter vegetable is "à la Polonaise"—in the Polish style. Cook 2 pints (about 1 pound) Brussels sprouts and drain well. Meanwhile, lightly brown 2 tablespoons butter or margarine. Blend in ¼ cup fine dry bread crumbs, 2 tablespoons snipped parsley, and 1 hard-cooked egg, finely chopped. Spoon the crumb mixture over the hot sprouts and toss together lightly.

Saucy Brussels Sprouts (pictured on pages 4-5)

2 pints Brussels sprouts
½ cup chopped onion
2 tablespoons butter
1 tablespoon all-purpose flour
1 tablespoon brown sugar
½ teaspoon dry mustard
½ cup milk
1 cup dairy sour cream

Cook fresh Brussels sprouts as directed above; drain well. Meanwhile, in 8-inch skillet or medium saucepan cook chopped onion in butter till tender but not brown. Blend in flour, brown sugar, dry mustard, and 1 teaspoon salt. Stir in milk. Cook, stirring constantly, till thickened and bubbly. Blend in sour cream. Add cooked Brussels sprouts; stir gently to combine. Cook till heated through, but *do not boil*. Makes 6 to 8 servings.

Marinated Brussels Sprouts Appetizers

2 10-ounce packages frozen
    Brussels sprouts, cooked
Tangy Marinade
2 tablespoons thinly sliced
    green onion with tops

Drain sprouts; toss with Tangy Marinade and onion. Cover; chill 8 hours or overnight, stirring often. Drain to serve.

Tangy Marinade: Combine ½ cup tarragon vinegar; ½ cup cooking oil; 1 small clove garlic, minced; 1 tablespoon sugar; 1 teaspoon salt; and dash bottled hot pepper sauce.

Cabbage

Selecting: *Popular cabbage varieties, available year-round, include the smooth-leafed green cabbage, crinkle-leafed Savoy green cabbage, and red cabbage. Look for firm, solid heads that feel heavy for their size. The leaves should be bright and free of blemishes. Store cabbage in a plastic bag in refrigerator crisper. Most varieties keep at least a week.*

Preparing: *Remove any wilted outer leaves; wash cabbage. Cut into wedges; remove center core. For shredded cabbage, hold wedge firmly and cut into even shreds with a sharp knife. To make short, fine shreds for a juicy slaw, finely chop shredded cabbage or use a shredder.*

Cooking: *In uncovered pan cook cabbage in small amount of boiling salted water for the first few minutes, then cover pan and cook till crisp-tender. Cook wedges 10 to 12 minutes; shredded cabbage 5 to 7 minutes. When cooking red cabbage, add a little lemon juice or vinegar to the water to prevent discoloring.*

Serving: *Use raw cabbage in coleslaw or any tossed salad. Cook cabbage with corned beef and other vegetables for the traditional New England boiled dinner.*

Coleslaw

3 cups shredded cabbage
⅓ cup chopped green pepper
⅓ cup mayonnaise *or* salad
    dressing
1 tablespoon vinegar
1 teaspoon sugar
½ teaspoon caraway seed

Combine shredded cabbage and chopped green pepper. Blend together mayonnaise or salad dressing, vinegar, sugar, caraway seed, and ¼ teaspoon salt. Toss mayonnaise mixture with vegetables. Cover and chill. Makes 6 servings.

Pennsylvania Red Cabbage

2 tablespoons bacon drippings
¼ cup packed brown sugar
¼ cup vinegar
½ teaspoon caraway seed
4 cups shredded red cabbage
2 cups cubed unpeeled apple

Heat bacon drippings in a skillet. Stir in brown sugar, vinegar, caraway seed, ¼ cup water, 1¼ teaspoons salt, and dash pepper. Add red cabbage and apple, stirring to coat. Cover and cook over low heat, stirring occasionally. For crisp cabbage, cook 15 minutes; for tender cabbage, cook 25 to 30 minutes. Makes 4 or 5 servings.

A superb variation of a cherished old-time recipe, *Cabbage and Ham Slaw* is sure to become a family favorite. The hollowed-out cabbage shell makes an eye-catching serving bowl.

Cabbage and Ham Slaw

2 tablespoons all-purpose flour
2 tablespoons sugar
1 teaspoon salt
1 teaspoon dry mustard
½ teaspoon celery seed
1 cup milk
2 slightly beaten egg yolks
3 tablespoons vinegar
2 tablespoons lemon juice
1 large head cabbage
2 cups cubed fully cooked ham
1 apple, cored and cut in thin
**   wedges**
¼ cup chopped green pepper
¼ cup sliced radish

In saucepan combine flour, sugar, salt, dry mustard, and celery seed; gradually blend in milk. Cook, stirring constantly, till thickened and bubbly. Stir half of the hot mixture into egg yolks; return to hot mixture in saucepan. Cook, stirring constantly, over low heat for 1 minute more. Stir in vinegar and lemon juice; cool.

Spread apart outer leaves of cabbage. Carefully cut out the center, leaving a ½-inch-thick shell to form a "bowl." Shred the removed cabbage to make 4 cups; toss with ham, apple, green pepper, and radish. Toss with cooked mixture; serve in cabbage shell. Makes 6 servings.

Stuffed Cabbage Rolls

½ cup chopped onion
2 tablespoons butter
3 cups cooked rice
¼ cup snipped parsley
12 large cabbage leaves
1 24-ounce can vegetable juice
   cocktail
1 tablespoon sugar
   Dairy sour cream
   Snipped parsley *or* crumbled,
    crisp-cooked bacon

Cook onion in butter till tender. Combine with rice and the ¼ cup parsley. Cut about 2 inches of heavy center vein out of cabbage leaves. Immerse leaves in boiling water just till limp, about 3 minutes; drain. Sprinkle generously with salt. Place about ¼ *cup* of the rice mixture in center of *each* leaf; fold in sides. Fold ends so they overlap atop rice. Place, seam side down, in 12x7½x2-inch baking dish. Combine vegetable juice cocktail and sugar; pour over cabbage rolls. Bake, covered, at 350° for 1 hour. Before serving, garnish with sour cream. Sprinkle with the additional parsley or the crumbled bacon. Makes 6 servings.

Perfection Salad

1 6-ounce package lemon-flavored
   gelatin
⅓ cup white vinegar
2 tablespoons lemon juice
2 cups finely shredded cabbage
1 cup chopped celery
½ cup chopped green pepper
¼ cup sliced pimiento-stuffed
   green olives
   Lettuce

Combine lemon gelatin and ¾ teaspoon salt. Add 3¼ cups boiling water; stir to dissolve gelatin. Stir in vinegar and lemon juice. Chill till mixture is partially set.

  Fold in shredded cabbage, celery, green pepper, and olives. Turn mixture into a 5½-cup mold or ten ½-cup molds. Chill till set. Unmold salad onto lettuce. Serve with mayonnaise or salad dressing, if desired. Makes 10 servings.

Mustard-Sauced Cabbage Wedges

1 small head cabbage
2 tablespoons finely chopped
   onion
2 tablespoons butter
1 tablespoon all-purpose flour
1 5⅓-ounce can evaporated milk
1 tablespoon prepared mustard
2 teaspoons prepared horseradish

Cut cabbage into 4 wedges; cook as directed on page 23. Drain well. Meanwhile, in small saucepan cook onion in butter till tender. Blend in flour, ¼ teaspoon salt, and dash pepper. Add evaporated milk and ½ cup water. Cook and stir till thickened and bubbly. Stir in mustard and horseradish. Spoon sauce over cabbage wedges. Sprinkle with snipped parsley, if desired. Makes 4 servings.

Sauerkraut

5 pounds fully matured cabbage,
   quartered, cored, and finely
   shredded
3½ tablespoons salt
   Cold water

Sprinkle cabbage with salt; mix well. Let stand 30 to 60 minutes. Firmly pack into clean, room-temperature jars; leave 2-inch headspace. Fill with cold water; leave ½-inch headspace. Prepare lids according to manufacturer's directions. Adjust lid on jar; screw band tight. Place jars on pan to catch brine that overflows. Set in cool place. Keep cabbage covered with brine. If necessary, open jars and add more brine made by dissolving 1½ tablespoons salt in 1 quart water. Sauerkraut is ready to can in 6 to 8 weeks.

  Wipe jar rim; replace lid if sealer appears damaged. Screw band tight. Set jars in water bath canner filled with cold water (should extend 2 inches above jars). Bring slowly to boil. Process pints or quarts for 30 minutes. Makes 7 pints.

Carrots

Selecting: Look for firm, well-shaped, bright golden carrots. Avoid carrots that are shriveled, soft, or cracked. Cut off any tops, then store carrots in refrigerator crisper in a plastic bag for as long as four weeks.

Preparing: Wash and trim carrots. If desired, scrub with a stiff brush, or peel. Leave tiny carrots whole. For larger carrots, dice, slice, shred, or cut into strips.

Cooking: Place carrots in a saucepan containing 1 inch of boiling salted water. Cover pan and cook till just tender (allow about 5 minutes for shredded carrots; 10 to 20 minutes for carrot strips or sliced, diced, or tiny whole carrots).

Serving: Crisp raw carrots are perfect vegetable dippers and enhance tossed and gelatin salads and relish trays. Shredded raw carrots and raisins tossed with mayonnaise or salad dressing make a delicious salad. For an easy vegetable dish, glaze cooked carrots with melted orange marmalade or a granulated or brown sugar-butter mixture.

Sunshine Carrots (pictured on page 29)

7 or 8 medium carrots
1 tablespoon granulated sugar *or* brown sugar
1 teaspoon cornstarch
¼ teaspoon ground ginger
¼ cup orange juice
2 tablespoons butter

Bias-slice carrots crosswise about ½ inch thick. Cook as directed above; drain. Meanwhile, in small saucepan combine sugar, cornstarch, ginger, and ¼ teaspoon salt. Add orange juice; cook, stirring constantly, till thickened and bubbly. Boil 1 minute; remove from heat. Stir in butter. Pour over hot carrots, tossing to coat evenly. Garnish with parsley and orange twist, if desired. Makes 6 servings.

Zesty Vegetable Salad (pictured on pages 4-5)

3 medium carrots
3 medium turnips
½ small head cauliflower, broken into flowerets (1½ cups)
1 small green pepper, cut into strips (½ cup)
½ cup vinegar
⅓ cup sugar
¼ cup salad oil
2 teaspoons curry powder

Peel and slice carrots and turnips; halve turnip slices. In saucepan combine carrots, turnips, cauliflower, green pepper, 2 cups water, and 1 teaspoon salt. Bring to boiling; reduce heat. Cover and simmer till crisp-tender, about 5 minutes. Drain and cool vegetables.

In screw-top jar combine vinegar, sugar, oil, curry, 1 teaspoon salt, and ¼ teaspoon pepper. Cover and shake vigorously. Pour vinegar mixture over vegetables; toss lightly. Refrigerate several hours or overnight, stirring vegetable mixture occasionally. Makes 8 servings.

Carrot Cake

2 cups all-purpose flour
2 cups granulated sugar
1 teaspoon baking powder
1 teaspoon baking soda
1 teaspoon ground cinnamon
3 cups finely shredded carrot
1 cup cooking oil
4 eggs
  Cream Cheese Frosting
¼ cup chopped nuts

Stir together flour, sugar, baking powder, soda, cinnamon, and 1 teaspoon salt. Add carrot, oil, and eggs. Mix till moistened; beat at medium speed of electric mixer for 2 minutes. Pour into greased and floured 13x9x2-inch baking pan. Bake at 325° for 50 to 60 minutes. Cool thoroughly. Spread with Cream Cheese Frosting. Top with nuts.

Cream Cheese Frosting: Soften one 3-ounce package cream cheese and ¼ cup butter *or* margarine; beat together till fluffy. Slowly beat in 2 cups sifted powdered sugar till smooth. Stir in 1 teaspoon vanilla.

Garden Gold Soup

6 medium carrots, cut up
  (1 pound)
3 medium potatoes, peeled and
  cubed
3 ribs celery with leaves,
  cut up
2 medium onions, quartered
4 cups water
2 teaspoons instant chicken
  bouillon granules
¼ teaspoon dried dillweed
1 cup milk
¼ cup butter *or* margarine

Place ¼ of the vegetables and *1 cup* of the water in a blender container. Cover and blend till coarsely chopped. Transfer mixture to a large kettle. Repeat process 3 times, using remaining vegetables and water. Stir in bouillon granules, dillweed, 2½ teaspoons salt, and ¼ teaspoon pepper. Cover; simmer till tender, 45 to 60 minutes.

Place *half* of the cooked mixture in blender container. Cover; blend till smooth, about 1 minute. Repeat process with remaining mixture. (*Or,* force the hot cooked mixture through a food mill.) Return pureed mixture to kettle; stir in milk and butter. Cover; heat through. Serves 8.

Crockery cooker directions: Blend vegetables and water as above; transfer to an electric slow crockery cooker. Stir in bouillon and seasonings as above. Cover; cook on low-heat setting 10 to 12 hours. Blend cooked mixture as above. Return to cooker; turn to high-heat setting. Stir in milk and butter. Cover; heat through, 30 minutes.

Golden Carrot Bake

3 cups shredded carrot (1 pound)
⅔ cup long grain rice
½ teaspoon salt
2 cups shredded American cheese
1 cup milk
2 beaten eggs
2 tablespoons instant minced
  onion

In saucepan combine carrot, rice, salt, and 1½ cups water. Bring to boiling. Reduce heat and simmer, covered, 25 minutes. *Do not drain.* Stir in 1½ cups of the shredded cheese, milk, eggs, onion, and ¼ teaspoon pepper. Turn into 1½-quart casserole. Bake, uncovered, at 350° about 1 hour. Top with remaining ½ cup shredded cheese. Return to oven to melt cheese, about 2 minutes. Makes 6 servings.

Pickled Carrots

6 medium carrots (1 pound)
¾ cup sugar
¾ cup vinegar
¾ cup water
1 tablespoon mustard seed
2½ inches stick cinnamon, broken
3 whole cloves

Cut carrots into 3-inch lengths. Simmer in small amount of boiling water for 5 minutes. Drain; cut into thin sticks. Combine sugar, vinegar, water, and mustard seed. Tie cinnamon and cloves in cheesecloth bag; add to vinegar mixture. Simmer 10 minutes. Pour over carrots; cool. Cover and refrigerate for 8 hours or overnight. Remove cheesecloth bag and drain before serving. Makes 2 cups.

Cauliflower

Selecting: *Cauliflower's peak season is September through November, but it is available in most areas year-round. Appearance is the most helpful indicator for selecting cauliflower. Choose a heavy, compact, white or creamy white head that has bright green leaves. Sprinkle leaves with water, cover tightly, and store in refrigerator crisper up to a week.*

Preparing: *Wash cauliflower head and remove leaves and woody stem. If desired, break the head into flowerets.*

Cooking: *In covered pan cook in a small amount of boiling salted water till just tender when tested with a fork (allow 10 to 15 minutes for flowerets; about 20 minutes for the whole head). Overcooking, even for only a few minutes, causes cauliflower to turn dark and become strong-flavored, so test frequently.*

Serving: *Raw cauliflower is a tasty addition to tossed salads, relish trays, or a platter of vegetable dippers. For a crisp relish, marinate cooked cauliflowerets in a vinegar-and-herb mixture. Serve cooked cauliflower with a cheese sauce.*

Cauliflower Polonaise

1 medium head cauliflower
1 hard-cooked egg
1 tablespoon butter *or* margarine
¼ cup fine dry bread crumbs
1 tablespoon snipped parsley

Cook whole cauliflower as directed above, or break into flowerets and cook as directed above. Drain well. Finely chop hard-cooked egg. Heat butter till lightly browned; stir in crumbs, snipped parsley, and chopped egg. Spoon over cooked cauliflower. Makes 5 or 6 servings.

Italian-Dressed Cauliflower

1 tablespoon chopped onion
1 small clove garlic, minced
2 tablespoons Italian salad
   dressing
3 cups small cauliflowerets
2 tablespoons chopped green
   pepper
⅛ teaspoon dried basil, crushed
1 cup cherry tomatoes, halved

In 1½-quart saucepan cook onion and garlic in salad dressing till onion is tender, about 2 minutes. Add cauliflowerets, ¼ cup water, and ½ teaspoon salt. Cook, covered, over low heat for 10 minutes. Add green pepper; cook till cauliflower is tender, about 5 minutes more. Stir in basil. Add tomatoes; heat through. Makes 6 servings.

Carrot and cauliflower favorites include *Sunshine Carrots* (see recipe, page 26), colorful *Italian-Dressed Cauliflower,* and *Cauliflower with Cheese-Mushroom Sauce* (see recipe, page 30).

Cauliflower with Cheese-Mushroom Sauce (pictured on page 29)

1 **medium head cauliflower**
1½ **cups sliced fresh mushrooms**
(4 ounces) *or* **1 4-ounce can**
sliced mushrooms, drained
2 **tablespoons butter**
2 **tablespoons all-purpose flour**
Dash white pepper
1 **cup milk**
1 **cup shredded sharp American**
cheese (4 ounces)
1 **teaspoon prepared mustard**
1 **tablespoon snipped parsley**

Cook whole cauliflower as directed on page 28, or break into flowerets and cook as directed on page 28. Drain cauliflower thoroughly; keep warm.

Meanwhile, cook fresh mushrooms in butter till tender, about 4 minutes. (Or, if using canned mushrooms, set them aside and melt butter.) Blend flour, white pepper, and ¼ teaspoon salt into butter. Add milk all at once. Cook, stirring constantly, till thickened and bubbly. Stir in cheese and mustard. If using canned mushrooms, stir them into sauce. Heat till cheese melts. Place head of cauliflower on platter; spoon some of the sauce over. Pass remaining sauce. Or, pour all sauce over flowerets in a bowl. Sprinkle with parsley. Makes 6 servings.

Cauliflower-Ham Chowder

2 **cups sliced cauliflowerets**
1 **13¾-ounce can chicken broth**
1 **cup milk** *or* **light cream**
1 **10¾-ounce can condensed cream**
of potato soup
2 **tablespoons cornstarch**
⅛ **teaspoon white pepper**
2 **cups diced fully cooked ham**

In large covered saucepan cook cauliflower in chicken broth till almost tender, about 10 minutes. *Do not drain;* set aside. In bowl gradually add milk to soup; mix well. Slowly blend ¼ cup cold water into cornstarch and white pepper; stir into soup mixture. Pour soup mixture over cauliflower; cook and stir till thickened and bubbly. Stir in ham; simmer till hot, about 10 minutes. Garnish with sliced green onion with tops, if desired. Serves 5 or 6.

Cauliflower Scallop

1 **10¾-ounce can condensed cream**
of celery soup
½ **cup milk**
2 **slightly beaten eggs**
1 **cup shredded Cheddar cheese**
¾ **cup soft bread crumbs**
¼ **cup snipped parsley**
¼ **cup chopped pimiento**
1 **tablespoon instant minced**
onion
2 **10-ounce packages frozen cauli-**
flower, cooked and drained

Combine soup, milk, and eggs; stir in *half* of the cheese, bread crumbs, parsley, pimiento, onion, ½ teaspoon salt, and dash pepper. Chop cauliflower; stir into soup mixture. Turn into 10x6x2-inch baking dish. Bake at 350° for 35 minutes. Top with remaining shredded Cheddar cheese; bake 5 minutes more. Makes 6 to 8 servings.

Bermuda Salad Bowl

1 **small head cauliflower,**
broken into flowerets
½ **large Bermuda onion, sliced**
½ **cup sliced pimiento-stuffed**
green olives
⅔ **cup French salad dressing**
1 **small head lettuce, torn in**
bite-size pieces
½ **cup crumbled blue cheese**

Slice cauliflowerets into a large salad bowl. Separate onion slices into rings; add to cauliflower. Add olives. Pour dressing over; toss. Chill 30 minutes. Just before serving, add the lettuce and cheese; toss lightly. Pass extra French dressing, if desired. Makes 8 to 10 servings.

Celery & Celeriac

Selecting: The well-known celery is a stalk consisting of individual ribs, but the less familiar celeriac (celery root) is grown for its turnip-like root. Look for celery stalks with crisp, solid, medium-sized ribs. Avoid stalks that are blemished, discolored, or have wilted leaves. When shopping for celeriacs, choose small roots, since large ones tend to be woody and hollow.

Preparing: Separate celery ribs and trim leaves. Peel celeriacs before using.

Cooking: In covered pan cook sliced celery or celeriac in a small amount of boiling salted water till just tender (10 to 15 minutes for celery; about 10 minutes for celeriac).

Serving: Raw celery ribs are a favorite vegetable dipper or, when stuffed with a cheese or peanut butter mixture, a popular relish tray addition. Try cooked celery creamed or use it to add texture to dishes. Cooked celeriacs are flavorful substitutes for potatoes. The French serve strips of raw celeriac with a sharp-flavored rémoulade sauce as an appetizer.

Celeriac Sauté

2 small celeriacs (about 1 pound)
2 tablespoons butter *or* margarine
1 tablespoon snipped parsley

Peel celeriacs; cut into julienne strips. Cook as directed above; drain thoroughly.

In small saucepan heat butter till brown. Pour over cooked celeriac. Season to taste with salt and pepper. Sprinkle with snipped parsley. Makes 4 servings.

Celeriac Toss

2 small celeriacs (about 1 pound)
2 medium carrots, cut into julienne strips (about 1 cup)
1 large avocado, pitted, peeled, and chopped
⅔ cup French salad dressing
Lettuce cups

Peel and coarsely chop celeriacs; cook as directed above. Drain. In deep bowl combine celeriacs, carrots, and avocado. Pour French salad dressing over and toss to coat. Refrigerate 2 to 3 hours, stirring occasionally. Drain vegetables and spoon into lettuce cups. Makes 6 to 8 servings.

Celery Slaw

3 **cups very thinly sliced celery**
1 **tablespoon sugar**
1 **tablespoon salad oil**
1 **tablespoon white vinegar**
1 **tablespoon finely chopped onion**
½ **teaspoon salt**
¼ **teaspoon paprika**
⅛ **teaspoon pepper**
½ **cup dairy sour cream**
½ **cup shredded carrot (1 medium)**
Lettuce

In covered pan cook celery in small amount of boiling water till crisp-tender, about 5 minutes; drain well. In medium bowl combine sugar, salad oil, vinegar, onion, salt, paprika, and pepper. Blend in sour cream. Add celery and shredded carrot; toss lightly to mix. Chill. Serve in lettuce-lined bowl. Makes 6 servings.

Crisp Dilled Celery

3 **cups celery bias-sliced ¾ inch thick**
1 **medium green pepper, cut in strips**
⅓ **cup water**
2 **tablespoons chopped onion**
1 **teaspoon instant chicken bouillon granules**
½ **teaspoon dried dillweed**
¼ **teaspoon salt**
2 **tablespoons butter *or* margarine**

In saucepan combine sliced celery, green pepper strips, water, chopped onion, chicken bouillon granules, dillweed, and salt. Cover tightly; simmer till celery is crisp-tender, 8 to 10 minutes. Drain. Add butter or margarine, stirring till melted. Makes 6 servings.

Baked Celery with Almonds

1 **stalk celery**
2 **cups boiling water**
½ **teaspoon salt**
3 **tablespoons butter**
3 **tablespoons all-purpose flour**
1⅓ **cups milk**
3 **tablespoons toasted slivered almonds**
¼ **cup fine dry bread crumbs**
1 **tablespoon butter, melted**

Cut celery ribs into ½-inch slices (5 cups), reserving tops. Combine sliced celery, tops, boiling water, and salt. Cook till celery is tender, 12 to 15 minutes. Discard tops; drain, reserving ½ cup cooking liquid. Melt the 3 tablespoons butter. Blend in flour, ½ teaspoon salt, and ¼ teaspoon pepper. Add milk and reserved liquid. Cook and stir till thickened. Remove from heat. Stir in celery and *half* of the nuts. Turn into 1-quart casserole. Top with remaining nuts. Toss crumbs with melted butter; sprinkle atop. Bake at 350° till heated through, 20 to 25 minutes. Makes 4 servings.

Cream of Celery Soup

1½ **cups chopped celery**
⅓ **cup chopped onion**
1 **cup water**
3 **cups milk**
3 **tablespoons all-purpose flour**
⅛ **teaspoon white pepper**
2 **tablespoons butter *or* margarine**

In 2-quart saucepan combine celery, onion, and ½ teaspoon salt; add water. Cover and cook till vegetables are tender, about 15 minutes. *Do not drain.* Add 2½ *cups* of the milk. Blend the remaining ½ cup milk, the flour, white pepper, and ½ teaspoon salt; add to celery mixture. Cook, stirring constantly, till thickened and bubbly. Stir in butter or margarine. Season to taste with salt and pepper. If desired, garnish with snipped parsley. Makes 6 servings.

Corn

Selecting: The peak season for fresh sweet corn is during the summer. Choose ears of corn that are well filled with even rows of plump, milky kernels. Look for fresh, green husks and avoid ears that are wormy. For best flavor, use fresh corn right after picking or purchasing. If corn can't be used immediately, store it, unhusked, in the coolest part of the refrigerator. If storage space is limited, you may husk the ears and place them in a plastic bag before refrigerating.

Preparing: Remove husks; scrub with a stiff brush to remove silks; rinse. For cut corn, use a sharp knife to cut off just the kernel tips, then scrape the cob with dull edge of knife.

Cooking: Cook ears of corn in a covered pan in a small amount of boiling salted water till just done, 6 to 8 minutes. Or, cook in uncovered pan in enough boiling salted water to cover ears. For foil-baked corn, spread ears with butter and sprinkle with salt and pepper. Wrap corn in foil; bake at 450° about 25 minutes. Turn several times during baking. For cut corn, cook in a covered pan in a small amount of boiling salted water or milk till done, 12 to 15 minutes.

Green Corn Pudding

4 fresh ears of corn
3 egg yolks
2 tablespoons sugar
2 tablespoons butter, melted
2 cups milk
3 stiffly beaten egg whites

With sharp knife, make cuts *through center* of kernels. Scrape cob. Measure 1¾ cups corn. Beat egg yolks till thick and lemon-colored. Stir in corn, sugar, butter, and 1 teaspoon salt. Slowly beat in milk. Fold in egg whites. Bake in 8x8x2-inch baking dish at 350° till knife inserted off-center comes out clean, 45 to 50 minutes. Serves 6 to 8.

Baked Corn with Chive Sauce

2 12-ounce cans whole kernel corn, drained
1 4-ounce container whipped cream cheese with chives

In a 1-quart casserole combine whole kernel corn, cream cheese with chives, ¼ teaspoon salt, and dash pepper. Cover and bake at 325° about 45 minutes. Serve baked corn in sauce dishes. Makes 6 servings.

Swiss Corn Bake (see recipe, page 36) is equally delicious made with commercially-canned corn
as with *Home-Canned Whole Kernel Corn. Home-Canned Cream-Style Corn* is another vegetable favorite.

Two-Corn Bread

1 cup all-purpose flour
1 cup yellow cornmeal
2 tablespoons sugar
1 tablespoon baking powder
3 eggs
1 cup cream-style cottage cheese
1 8-ounce can cream-style corn

Stir together flour, cornmeal, sugar, baking powder, and ¼ teaspoon salt. Beat eggs and cottage cheese till smooth; stir in corn. Add to dry ingredients; stir just till blended. Turn into greased 9x9x2-inch baking pan. Bake at 375° for 30 to 35 minutes. Serve warm. Makes 9 servings.

Home-Canned Whole Kernel Corn

Fresh ears of corn (allow 3 to 6 pounds for each quart)
Salt (¼ teaspoon for each pint; ½ teaspoon for each quart)
Boiling water

Cut corn from cob at ⅔'s depth; do not scrape cob. For *raw pack,* pack corn loosely into hot, clean jars; leave 1-inch headspace. Add salt. Cover corn with boiling water; leave 1-inch headspace. For *hot pack,* add 2 cups boiling water per 1 quart corn; bring to boil. Pack loosely into hot, clean jars; leave 1-inch headspace. Add salt and boiling cooking liquid; leave 1-inch headspace. Prepare lids according to manufacturer's directions. Wipe jar rim. Adjust lid on jar. Process raw or hot pack corn in *pressure canner* at 10 pounds pressure for 55 minutes for pints; 85 minutes for quarts. Boil corn 20 minutes *before* tasting or using.

Home-Canned Cream-Style Corn

Fresh ears of corn (allow 1½ to 3 pounds for each pint)
Salt (¼ teaspoon for each pint)
Boiling water

Cut corn from cob, cutting only about half the kernel; then scrape cob. For *raw pack,* pack corn loosely into hot, clean pint jars, leaving 1-inch headspace. Add salt. Fill jars with boiling water, leaving 1-inch headspace. For *hot pack,* cover corn with boiling water; bring to a boil. Pack loosely into hot, clean pint jars, leaving 1-inch headspace. Add salt. Prepare lids according to manufacturer's directions. Wipe off rim of jar. Adjust lid on jar.

Process raw pack corn in *pressure canner* at 10 pounds pressure for 95 minutes for pints. *Process hot pack* corn in *pressure canner* at 10 pounds pressure for 85 minutes for pints. Boil corn 20 minutes *before* tasting or using.

Pressure Canning is Essential

All vegetables—except tomatoes or those made into pickles, relishes, or sauerkraut—are susceptible to botulism. They *must be pressure-canned* to reach the high temperature needed to destroy botulism-causing organisms. When using a pressure canner, read and follow the manufacturer's directions thoroughly. At 10 pounds pressure, the temperature reaches 240° at sea level (versus 212° in a boiling water bath). The processing time in the recipe ensures adequate heat penetration. In high-altitude areas, over 2,000 feet, check with a county extension agent for corrections. *Never* serve home-canned vegetables cold from the jar. Boil corn or spinach 20 minutes (others at least 10 minutes) before tasting or using.

Swiss Corn Bake (pictured on page 34)

1 pint Home-Canned Whole Kernel
   Corn (see page 35) *or*
   1 16-ounce can whole kernel
   corn, drained
1 5⅓-ounce can evaporated milk
1 cup shredded process Swiss
   cheese (4 ounces)
2 beaten eggs
2 tablespoons finely chopped
   onion
1 cup soft bread crumbs
2 tablespoons butter, melted

Boil home-canned corn, uncovered, 20 minutes *before* tasting or using. Drain well. Combine corn, evaporated milk, ¾ *cup* of the shredded cheese, eggs, chopped onion, and dash pepper. Turn mixture into a 10x6x2-inch baking dish or a 1-quart casserole. Toss bread crumbs with the melted butter and the remaining ¼ cup shredded cheese. Sprinkle over corn mixture. Bake at 350° for 25 to 30 minutes. Garnish with green pepper rings, if desired. Makes 4 to 6 servings.

Corn Medley

1 10-ounce package frozen whole
   kernel corn
½ cup chopped celery
1 teaspoon instant chicken
   bouillon granules
1 2½-ounce jar sliced mushrooms
1 medium tomato

In saucepan combine corn, celery, bouillon granules, and ⅓ cup water. Bring to boiling; reduce heat. Cover and simmer till vegetables are tender, 5 to 7 minutes. Drain mushrooms. Cut tomato into thin wedges. Stir mushrooms and tomato wedges into corn mixture; heat through. Season to taste with salt and pepper. Makes 6 servings.

Roasted Corn on the Cob

½ cup butter *or* margarine,
   softened
1 teaspoon salt
½ teaspoon dried rosemary,
   crushed
½ teaspoon dried marjoram,
   crushed
6 fresh ears of corn in husks

Cream together butter and salt till fluffy. Combine herbs and blend into butter. Keep butter at room temperature for 1 hour to mellow. Turn back husks of corn; remove silks with a stiff brush. Place each ear on a piece of heavy-duty foil. Spread corn with about *1 tablespoon* of the butter mixture. Lay husks back in position. Wrap corn securely with foil. Roast ears directly on *hot* coals; turn frequently till corn is tender, 12 to 15 minutes. Or, if you have a covered grill with an elevated rack, roast corn according to manufacturer's directions. Makes 6 servings.

Corn Relish

1 10-ounce package frozen whole
   kernel corn
½ cup sugar
1 tablespoon cornstarch
½ cup vinegar
2 tablespoons finely chopped
   celery
2 tablespoons finely chopped
   green pepper
2 tablespoons chopped pimiento
1 tablespoon minced onion
1 teaspoon ground turmeric
½ teaspoon dry mustard

Cook corn according to package directions; drain. In saucepan combine sugar and cornstarch; stir in vinegar and ⅓ cup cold water. Stir in corn, celery, green pepper, pimiento, onion, turmeric, and dry mustard. Cook, stirring constantly, till thickened and bubbly; cook and stir 3 to 4 minutes more. Cover and chill thoroughly. Makes 2 cups.

Scalloped Corn

1 beaten egg
1 cup milk
1 cup coarsely crushed saltine
   crackers (22 crackers)
¾ teaspoon salt
   Dash pepper
1 17-ounce can cream-style corn
¼ cup finely chopped onion
3 tablespoons chopped pimiento
1 tablespoon butter, melted

Combine egg, milk, ⅔ cup of the cracker crumbs, salt, and pepper. Stir in corn, onion, and pimiento; mix well. Turn into 1-quart casserole. Toss melted butter with the remaining ⅓ cup cracker crumbs; sprinkle atop corn mixture. Bake at 350° for 65 to 70 minutes. Makes 6 servings.

Parsley Buttered Corn

6 fresh ears of corn
½ cup butter or margarine,
   softened
1 tablespoon snipped parsley
1 teaspoon lemon juice
⅛ teaspoon salt
⅛ teaspoon dried savory, crushed
   Dash pepper

Cook ears of corn in boiling salted water as directed on page 33. Cream butter. Blend in parsley, lemon juice, salt, savory, and pepper. Serve with corn. Makes 6 servings.
Microwave cooking directions: Wrap each ear of corn in waxed paper; twist ends of paper to seal. Arrange corn on paper toweling, allowing at least 1 inch between ears. Cook corn in countertop microwave oven for 8 to 10 minutes for six ears. (Allow 2 minutes for one ear; 3 to 4 minutes for two ears; and 6 to 7 minutes for four ears.) Halfway through cooking, rearrange corn and turn over. Prepare butter mixture as above and serve with corn.

Fresh Creamed Corn

5 fresh ears of corn
2 slices bacon
½ cup milk
½ teaspoon sugar
½ teaspoon salt
   Dash pepper
½ cup light cream
1½ teaspoons all-purpose flour
1 tablespoon butter or margarine

Cut corn from cob; set aside. In an 8-inch skillet cook bacon till crisp; remove and crumble, reserving drippings. Add corn, milk, sugar, salt, and pepper to reserved drippings. Cover and cook 15 to 20 minutes, stirring occasionally. In screw-top jar shake together light cream and flour till combined; stir into corn mixture. Add butter or margarine. Cook, stirring constantly, till thickened and bubbly. Garnish with crumbled bacon. Makes 6 servings.

Fresh Corn Chowder

6 fresh ears of corn
⅓ cup water
¼ cup chopped onion
½ teaspoon salt
4 cups milk
2 tablespoons butter
1 teaspoon salt
¼ teaspoon white pepper
3 tablespoons all-purpose flour
1 beaten egg

With sharp knife, make cuts through center of kernels. Cut corn off cob; scrape cob. In saucepan combine corn, water, onion, and the ½ teaspoon salt. Bring to a boil. Reduce heat and simmer, covered, 15 minutes, stirring occasionally. Stir in 3½ cups of the milk, butter, the 1 teaspoon salt, and white pepper. Blend together remaining ½ cup milk and flour; stir into corn mixture. Cook and stir till thickened and bubbly. Gradually stir about 1 cup of the hot mixture into egg; return to hot mixture in saucepan. Cook over low heat, stirring constantly, for 2 minutes more. Garnish with snipped chives and paprika, if desired. Makes 6 servings.

Cucumbers

Selecting: Choose firm, bright or dark green, well-shaped cucumbers. Pass up those that have an overgrown, puffy appearance and yellowing rind. Cucumbers 6 to 9 inches in length are best suited for slicing and recipe use. Smaller 1- to 4-inch cucumbers are preferred for pickles. Cucumbers keep fresh up to two weeks stored in the refrigerator.

Preparing: Scrub cucumbers. The cucumber peel is edible and adds color to most recipes, but this vegetable may be peeled if desired. For pretty frilled slices, run the tines of a fork lengthwise along the unpeeled cucumber before slicing.

Tip: To keep the cucumber crisp, very thinly slice the vegetable and place in ice water immediately after cutting.

Serving: Add cucumbers to tossed salads, molded salads, and relish trays, or combine them with onion slices in a vinegar or sour cream dressing. Whether your preference is dill or sweet, cucumber pickles are an all-time favorite.

Cucumbers in Sour Cream

2 medium cucumbers, thinly
   sliced
1 medium onion, thinly sliced
½ cup dairy sour cream
1 tablespoon sugar
1 tablespoon vinegar

Combine the cucumbers and onion. Stir together sour cream, sugar, vinegar, and ½ teaspoon salt; toss with vegetables. Cover and chill, stirring occasionally. Makes 3 cups.

Quick Mustard Pickles

2½ to 3 pounds cucumbers
1½ cups vinegar
1 cup water
1 cup sugar
1 4-ounce jar prepared mustard
   (½ cup)
2 teaspoons salt
1 teaspoon prepared horseradish

Cut cucumbers into ½-inch chunks or ¼-inch slices. Measure 8 cups. In large saucepan mix vinegar, water, sugar, mustard, salt, and horseradish; bring to boil. Pack cucumbers into hot, clean pint jars; pour boiling liquid over cucumbers, leaving ½-inch headspace. (Liquid will be cloudy due to mustard.) Prepare lids according to manufacturer's directions. Wipe jar rim. Adjust lid on jar. Process in boiling water bath 5 minutes. (Start timing when water returns to boil.) Mustard may settle during standing. Makes 4 pints.

Refreshing *Cucumber Ring Supreme* wreathed with fresh watercress and garnished
with colorful cherry tomatoes is the perfect salad choice for a summer buffet or luncheon menu.

Cucumber Ring Supreme

  1 tablespoon sugar
1½ teaspoons unflavored gelatin
  ½ teaspoon salt
  2 tablespoons lemon juice
  ½ cucumber, thinly sliced
  2 tablespoons sugar
  1 envelope unflavored gelatin
  ¾ teaspoon salt
  2 tablespoons lemon juice
  1 8-ounce package cream cheese,
     cubed and softened
    About 6 medium cucumbers,
     peeled
  1 cup mayonnaise *or* salad
     dressing
  ¼ cup snipped parsley
  3 tablespoons finely chopped
     onion

In small saucepan combine the 1 tablespoon sugar, the 1½ teaspoons unflavored gelatin, and the ½ teaspoon salt. Stir in ¾ cup water; stir over low heat till gelatin and sugar are dissolved. Stir in 2 tablespoons lemon juice. Pour into 6½-cup ring mold. Chill till partially set. Overlay the thinly sliced cucumber atop gelatin mixture in mold; press into gelatin. Chill till *almost* firm.

Meanwhile, in saucepan mix the 2 tablespoons sugar, the 1 envelope unflavored gelatin, and the ¾ teaspoon salt. Add ⅔ cup water; stir over low heat till gelatin and sugar are dissolved. Stir in 2 tablespoons lemon juice. Gradually beat hot gelatin mixture into softened cream cheese with rotary beater till mixture is smooth.

Halve the 6 cucumbers and scrape out seeds; grind using fine blade, or finely shred. Measure 2 cups drained ground cucumber. Fold ground cucumber, mayonnaise, parsley, and onion into cream cheese mixture. Pour over almost firm gelatin in mold. Chill till firm. Makes 8 servings.

Dill Pickles

For each quart:
½ pound 4-inch cucumbers
   (5 or 6 cucumbers)
3 or 4 heads fresh dill
1 teaspoon mustard seed
2 cups water
1 cup cider vinegar
1 tablespoon pickling salt

Pack cucumbers loosely in hot, clean quart jars, leaving ½-inch headspace. Add dill and mustard seed to each quart. Make a brine by combining water, vinegar, and salt. Bring to boiling. Slowly pour hot brine over cucumbers, leaving ½-inch headspace. Prepare lids according to manufacturer's directions. Wipe jar rim. Adjust lid on jar. Process in boiling water bath for 20 minutes (start timing as soon as jars are placed in water).

   Kosher Dill Pickles: Pack cucumbers in quart jars as above. Add dill to each quart; *omit* the mustard seed. Add 1 clove garlic and 1 small piece hot red pepper (optional) to each quart. Prepare a brine using 2¼ cups water, ¾ cup vinegar, and 1 tablespoon pickling salt. Bring to boiling. Slowly pour hot brine over cucumbers, leaving ½-inch headspace. Prepare lids and process as above.

Crisp Pickle Slices

4 quarts sliced cucumbers
6 medium onions, sliced
   (6 cups)
2 green peppers, sliced
   (1⅔ cups)
3 cloves garlic
⅓ cup pickling salt
   Cracked ice
5 cups sugar
3 cups cider vinegar
2 tablespoons mustard seed
1½ teaspoons ground turmeric
1½ teaspoons celery seed

Combine sliced cucumbers, onions, green peppers, garlic (speared on wooden picks for easy removal), and pickling salt. Cover with cracked ice; mix well. Let cucumber mixture stand for 3 hours; drain well. Remove garlic. Combine sugar, cider vinegar, mustard seed, turmeric, and celery seed; pour over cucumber mixture. Bring to boiling. Pack cucumbers and liquid into hot, clean pint jars, leaving ½-inch headspace. Prepare lids according to manufacturer's directions. Wipe jar rim. Adjust lid on jar. Process jars in boiling water bath for 5 minutes. (Start timing when water returns to boiling.) Makes 8 pints.

Pickle-making Pointers

● Choose a cucumber variety developed just for pickling.
● Make pickles out of cucumbers within 24 hours of harvesting. Cucumbers that are held longer may produce a hollow or soft pickle.
● Use pure granulated pickling salt or uniodized table salt. Iodized table salt causes pickles to darken.
● Choose a high-grade vinegar of 4- to 6-percent acid (40 to 60 grain). Never dilute the vinegar more than specified in the recipe.
● Use herbs and spices from newly opened packages.
● Use soft water for pickles. Minerals in hard water settle in the bottom of the jar after processing.
● Choose utensils made of stoneware, aluminum, glass, or stainless steel.
● Pack pickles in standard canning jars.
● Process pickles in water bath canner. The processing destroys organisms that cause spoilage.

Eggplant

Selecting: This pear-shaped vegetable is most plentiful in August and September, although it's available in most supermarkets throughout the year. Look for a firm, heavy eggplant with a dark, shiny, smooth skin and a fresh-looking, green cap. Avoid those that have dark spots, which indicate decay, or feel spongy. Store in refrigerator up to two weeks.

Preparing: Wash, cut off the cap, and, if desired, peel the eggplant.

Cooking: For freshest flavor, sauté eggplant in oil, bake it, broil it, or cook in a small amount of boiling salted water. Avoid boiling in a large amount of water. A well-cooked eggplant has a tender and moist interior that's not wet or soggy.

Serving: For a tasty main dish, stuff eggplant with a meat filling or use sliced or cubed eggplant in casseroles. Serve sautéed eggplant with a rich tomato sauce for a delicious vegetable dish. Team cubed eggplant and your favorite meat for special kabobs. Or, try deep-fat fried eggplant strips as an unusual snack or appetizer.

Jackstraw Eggplant

1 medium eggplant, peeled
1 cup all-purpose flour
1 cup ice water
1 slightly beaten egg
2 tablespoons cooking oil
½ teaspoon sugar
  Fat for deep-fat frying
  Grated Parmesan cheese

Halve eggplant lengthwise; cut crosswise into ½-inch slices. Cut slices into ½-inch strips. Beat together flour, ice water, egg, oil, sugar, and ½ teaspoon salt. Dip eggplant strips in batter, allowing excess to drain off. Fry, a few at a time, in deep hot fat (365°) for 4 to 5 minutes. Drain on paper toweling. Sprinkle with additional salt. Serve hot with Parmesan cheese.

Panfried Eggplant

1 medium eggplant, peeled
1 slightly beaten egg
½ cup finely crushed rich
    round crackers
2 tablespoons snipped parsley
½ cup cooking oil

Halve eggplant lengthwise, then cut crosswise into ½-inch slices. Combine egg and 1 tablespoon water. Combine crackers, parsley, ½ teaspoon salt, and ⅛ teaspoon pepper. Dip eggplant in egg mixture, then in cracker mixture. Cook eggplant in hot oil till tender and golden, 2 to 3 minutes per side. Drain on paper toweling. Serves 4 to 6.

The Greek specialty *Moussaka* features tender slices of eggplant nestled in a cinnamon custard mixture. Layered beneath are more eggplant and wine-tomato sauced ground lamb or beef.

Moussaka

2 large eggplants, peeled and
   cut into ½-inch slices
¼ cup cooking oil
2 pounds ground lamb *or* ground
   beef
1 cup chopped onion
1 clove garlic, minced
1 8-ounce can tomato sauce
¾ cup dry red wine
2 tablespoons snipped parsley
¼ teaspoon dried oregano,
   crushed
¼ teaspoon ground cinnamon
1 beaten egg
¼ cup butter *or* margarine
¼ cup all-purpose flour
2 cups milk
3 beaten eggs
½ cup grated Parmesan cheese
   Ground cinnamon

Brush both sides of eggplant slices with the oil; sprinkle with salt. In large skillet brown eggplant slices, about 1½ minutes on each side. Drain and set aside. In same skillet cook lamb or beef, onion, and garlic till meat is brown and onion is tender; drain off excess fat. Stir in tomato sauce, wine, parsley, oregano, the ¼ teaspoon cinnamon, and 1 teaspoon salt. Simmer, uncovered, for 10 minutes. Gradually stir mixture into the 1 beaten egg.

Meanwhile, in a saucepan melt butter or margarine; stir in flour, 1 teaspoon salt, and dash pepper. Add milk all at once; cook and stir till thickened and bubbly. Gradually stir the hot sauce into the 3 beaten eggs.

In 13x9x2-inch baking dish arrange *half* the eggplant. Pour all the meat mixture over; top with remaining eggplant. Pour milk mixture over all. Top with Parmesan and additional cinnamon. Bake at 325° for 40 to 45 minutes. Top with more parsley, if desired. Makes 8 to 10 servings.

Eggplant Parmigiana

¼ cup all-purpose flour
½ teaspoon salt
1 medium eggplant, peeled and
   cut into ½-inch slices
1 beaten egg
½ cup cooking oil
⅓ cup grated Parmesan cheese
   Homemade Tomato Sauce
1 6-ounce package sliced
   mozzarella cheese

Combine flour and salt. Dip eggplant into beaten egg, then in flour mixture. In large skillet brown eggplant in hot oil; drain well on paper toweling. Place 1 layer of eggplant in 10x6x2-inch baking dish, cutting slices to fit. Sprinkle with *half* the Parmesan. Top with *half* the Homemade Tomato Sauce and *half* the mozzarella. Cut remaining mozzarella into triangles. Repeat eggplant, Parmesan, Homemade Tomato Sauce, and mozzarella layers. Bake at 400° till heated through, 15 to 20 minutes. Makes 6 servings.

Homemade Tomato Sauce: In saucepan cook ⅓ cup chopped onion; ¼ cup finely chopped celery; ½ clove garlic, minced; and 1 teaspoon dried parsley flakes in 2 tablespoons olive oil *or* cooking oil till onion and celery are tender but not brown. Stir in one 16-ounce can Italian tomatoes; ⅓ cup tomato paste; ½ teaspoon salt; ½ teaspoon dried oregano, crushed; ¼ teaspoon pepper, and 1 bay leaf. Simmer gently, uncovered, 45 to 50 minutes. Remove bay leaf.

Stuffed Eggplant

1 large eggplant (1½ pounds)
¼ cup chopped onion
1 tablespoon butter *or* margarine
1 10¾-ounce can condensed
   cream of mushroom soup
1 tablespoon snipped parsley
½ teaspoon Worcestershire sauce
1 cup finely crushed rich round
   crackers (24 crackers)

Cut a thin slice off one side of eggplant. Remove pulp to within ½-inch of skin. Cook pulp in small amount of boiling water till tender, about 10 minutes; drain well. Cook onion in butter till tender. Stir in eggplant pulp, soup, parsley, and Worcestershire. Set aside 2 tablespoons crushed crackers; stir remaining crackers into onion mixture. Fill eggplant shell with mixture. Place in 10x6x2-inch baking dish; sprinkle reserved crumbs over top. Carefully pour hot water in bottom of dish to depth of ½ inch. Bake at 375° till heated through, 50 to 60 minutes. Serves 4 to 6.

Greens

Selecting: The green leaves and, sometimes, stems of plants have been used as vegetables for hundreds of years. Turnip greens, collard greens, mustard greens, beet greens, dandelion greens, kale, and chard or Swiss chard are all greens. Choose fresh-looking, crisp greens that are free of insect injury. For best quality, use greens the same day as purchased.

Preparing: Thoroughly wash greens in cool water to remove dirt and sand particles. Cut off any roots and remove damaged portions and large veins. Tear or cut up large leaves.

Cooking: Greens need to be cooked in covered pan in boiling salted water only till tender, but cooking time varies from 10 minutes to 75 minutes depending on the type and maturity of the greens. Considerably longer cooking is typical in many recipes.

Serving: Raw greens are flavorful additions to tossed salads. Salt pork, butter, vinegar, and lemon juice are popular seasonings for cooked greens.

Sweet-Sour Swiss Chard

6 cups torn Swiss chard
6 slices bacon
½ cup sliced green onion with tops
4 teaspoons sugar
2 teaspoons all-purpose flour
⅓ cup water
¼ cup vinegar

Place chard in large salad bowl; set aside. In skillet cook bacon till crisp; drain, reserving ¼ cup bacon drippings. Crumble bacon; set aside. In same skillet cook onion in reserved drippings till tender but not brown. Blend in sugar, flour, and ½ teaspoon salt; stir in water and vinegar. Cook and stir till thickened and bubbly. Pour hot mixture over chard, tossing to coat. Sprinkle with bacon. Serve immediately. Makes 4 to 6 servings.

Salt Pork and Greens

½ pound salt pork
8 cups water
1½ pounds beet greens, turnip greens, Swiss chard, *or* mustard greens (about 16 cups)

Cut salt pork into thin strips. Place pork and water in kettle or Dutch oven; simmer, covered, for 45 minutes. Prepare greens as directed above; add to pork and water. Simmer, covered, 1 hour. Drain greens, reserving liquid. Season greens and pork with salt and pepper to taste. If desired, serve cooking liquid over. Makes 6 servings.

Garden-fresh turnips become a hearty vegetable dish when you prepare a big kettle of
the flavorful Southern favorite, *Turnip Greens with Cornmeal Dumplings* (see recipe, page 46).

Turnip Greens with Cornmeal Dumplings (pictured on page 45)

4 ounces salt pork with rind
2 pounds turnip greens
1 pound turnips
10 cups water
1 teaspoon salt
1½ cups cornmeal
½ cup all-purpose flour
1 teaspoon baking powder
1 teaspoon sugar
½ teaspoon salt
3 tablespoons butter *or*
    margarine, melted
1 beaten egg

Chop salt pork, cutting to, but not through, rind. Discard stems of greens and any damaged portions. Tear up large leaves (should have about 12 cups greens). Peel and quarter turnips. In large kettle bring water to boil. Add salt pork, greens, turnips, and 1 teaspoon salt. Simmer, covered, 2 hours. Remove 1 cup broth; reserve for dumplings. Remove and discard salt pork. Season remaining broth to taste.

For dumplings, in mixing bowl combine cornmeal, flour, baking powder, sugar, and the ½ teaspoon salt; stir together thoroughly. Stir in melted butter or margarine and the reserved 1 cup broth. Stir in beaten egg. Spoon batter by rounded tablespoonfuls onto simmering greens to make 12 dumplings. Cover and simmer 25 to 30 minutes. To serve, ladle greens and broth into soup bowls; top each serving with 2 dumplings. Makes 6 servings.

Sweet-Sour Kale

½ pound kale, mustard greens, *or*
    collard greens *or* 1 10-ounce
    package frozen chopped kale
    or collard greens
2 slices bacon
4 teaspoons all-purpose flour
¾ cup hot water
1 tablespoon sugar
1 tablespoon cider vinegar
¼ teaspoon salt
    Dash pepper

Cut roots off fresh kale or greens and remove any damaged portions. Cut stems and leaves into small pieces. In covered saucepan cook fresh kale or greens in large amount of boiling salted water till tender, 60 to 75 minutes. Drain well. (Or, cook frozen chopped kale or collard greens according to package directions; drain well.)

In skillet cook bacon till crisp. Remove bacon, reserving drippings in skillet. Crumble bacon and set aside. Blend flour into drippings. Add hot water; cook and stir till thickened and bubbly. Stir in sugar, cider vinegar, salt, and pepper. Stir in drained cooked kale or greens; heat through. Garnish with crumbled bacon. Makes 4 servings.

Ham Hocks 'n Greens

1 pound mustard greens
½ pound turnip greens
½ pound collard greens
4 cups water
3½ pounds ham hocks
    Corn Bread
    Hard-cooked egg slices
    (optional)

Discard stems of greens and any damaged portions. Tear up large leaves. In large kettle combine water and ham hocks; bring to boiling. Add mustard, turnip, and collard greens; return to boiling. Reduce heat; simmer, covered, 1½ hours.

About ½ hour before greens are done, prepare Corn Bread. To serve, ladle greens and juices (pot liquor) into bowl; garnish with hard-cooked egg slices, if desired. Offer ham hocks in another bowl. Pass Corn Bread. Makes 4 servings.

Corn Bread: In mixing bowl stir together 1 cup all-purpose flour, 1 cup yellow cornmeal, ¼ cup sugar, 4 teaspoons baking powder, and ¾ teaspoon salt. Add 1 cup milk, 2 eggs, and ¼ cup cooking oil. Beat with rotary beater or electric mixer just till smooth, about 1 minute; do not overbeat. Bake in greased 9x9x2-inch baking pan at 350° for 20 to 25 minutes. Cut into squares.

Kohlrabi

Selecting: *Although sometimes called cabbage turnip because of its appearance and flavor, kohlrabi is not a root vegetable; the edible globe forms above the ground. The plant grows well spring through fall, but marketable quantities are greatest in June and July. Choose globes that look fresh and unscarred. Those less than 3 inches in diameter are younger and usually milder in flavor. Leaves are edible too, but wilt quickly and are often trimmed off before sale. Kohlrabies will keep for several days in the refrigerator crisper.*
Preparing: *Peel off tough outer skin. Slice or chop the flesh according to planned use.*
Cooking: *In covered pan cook in small amount of boiling salted water till tender, about 25 minutes.*
Serving: *Serve raw on relish tray or in a salad. Serve cooked kohlrabi buttered or mashed with salt and pepper, or accented with other seasonings such as dry mustard, tarragon, or thyme.*

Kohlrabi Slaw

6 medium kohlrabies
2 apples, cored and chopped
1 tablespoon sliced green onion
   with tops
½ cup dairy sour cream
¼ cup creamy French salad
   dressing

Peel and coarsely shred kohlrabies (should have about 3 cups). In medium bowl combine kohlrabies, apples, and green onion. Stir together sour cream and French salad dressing; stir into kohlrabi mixture. Chill. Serve in lettuce-lined bowl, if desired. Makes 6 servings.

Kohlrabi-Carrot Bake

3 medium kohlrabies
4 medium carrots, bias-sliced
¼ cup chopped onion
2 tablespoons butter
2 tablespoons all-purpose flour
½ teaspoon salt
1½ cups milk
¼ cup snipped parsley
1 tablespoon lemon juice
¾ cup soft bread crumbs
1 tablespoon butter, melted

Peel and slice kohlrabies. In covered saucepan cook kohlrabies in small amount of boiling salted water 15 minutes. Add carrots; cover and continue cooking till vegetables are tender, 10 to 12 minutes more. Drain. In saucepan cook onion in the 2 tablespoons butter till tender but not brown. Blend in flour, salt, and dash pepper. Add milk all at once. Cook and stir till thickened and bubbly. Stir in cooked vegetables, parsley, and lemon juice. Turn into 1-quart casserole. Combine bread crumbs and the 1 tablespoon melted butter; sprinkle around edge of casserole. Bake at 350° till heated through, 20 to 25 minutes. Makes 6 servings.

Lettuce

Selecting: While bright, fresh-looking green leaves are signs of quality, each lettuce type has special characteristics. Shown clockwise: Iceberg lettuce, with a firm but not hard head, should give slightly when squeezed. Avoid heads with rust marks. Salad bowl and leaf lettuce have leaves clustered loosely around a stem. Some types are red-tipped. Look for soft, tender leaves free from wilt or decay. Bibb lettuce, a small cup-shaped head with soft textured leaves, is a butterhead variety. Its deep green outer leaves become almost white near the core. Romaine or Cos (shown cut lengthwise) has a long head of coarse, stiff leaves with heavy midribs. Select full, unblemished heads. Wash lettuce as below and store in a plastic bag in refrigerator crisper. Iceberg and romaine keep up to a week; others keep one or two days.

Preparing: Remove discolored or wilted leaves and the core. Rinse lettuce under cold running water and drain thoroughly.

Tip: To core iceberg lettuce, whack stem end on a counter. Twist the core and lift out.

24-Hour Vegetable Salad

    3 cups torn romaine
      Salt
      Pepper
      Sugar
 1½ cups shredded Swiss cheese
      (6 ounces)
    4 hard-cooked eggs, sliced
  ½ pound bacon, crisp-cooked,
      drained, and crumbled
      (10 or 11 slices)
    3 cups torn leaf lettuce
    1 10-ounce package frozen
      peas, thawed (2 cups)
  ¾ cup mayonnaise *or* salad
      dressing
    2 tablespoons sliced green
      onion with tops

Place romaine in bottom of large bowl; sprinkle with salt, pepper, and sugar. Top with *1 cup* of the cheese. Layer eggs atop cheese, standing some slices on edge, if desired. Sprinkle generously with salt. Next, layer in order *half* of the bacon, the leaf lettuce, and the peas. Spread mayonnaise or salad dressing over top, sealing to edge of bowl. Cover and chill 24 hours or overnight. Garnish with remaining cheese, remaining bacon, and green onion. Toss before serving. Makes 10 to 12 servings.

Lettuce salads usually have to be made at the last minute. This *24-Hour Vegetable Salad* is an exception. A creamy layer of mayonnaise seals in the flavor, and chilling keeps it crisp.

Chili-Pepperoni Salad Bowl

1 medium head iceberg lettuce
3 cups corn chips
4 ounces pepperoni, thinly
    sliced
1 large tomato, chopped
½ cup shredded Cheddar cheese
    (2 ounces)
¼ cup sliced pitted ripe olives
1 15-ounce can chili with beans

Line salad bowl with outer lettuce leaves; cut remaining lettuce into bite-size chunks. Place lettuce chunks, chips, pepperoni, tomato, cheese, and olives in bowl. Heat chili; pour atop salad. Toss lightly. Makes 6 servings.

Braised Lettuce

2 tablespoons finely chopped
    onion
2 tablespoons finely chopped
    carrot
1 tablespoon butter *or* margarine
½ cup water
2 teaspoons sugar
½ teaspoon instant chicken
    bouillon granules
½ teaspoon salt
1 medium head iceberg lettuce,
    shredded (6 cups)
½ of an 8-ounce can water chestnuts,
    drained and sliced
    Snipped parsley
    Toasted slivered almonds
    (optional)

In medium saucepan cook onion and carrot in butter or margarine till tender but not brown. Stir in water, sugar, bouillon granules, and salt; heat and stir till bouillon granules are dissolved. Add shredded lettuce and water chestnuts. Cover and simmer over low heat for 5 to 8 minutes. *Do not overcook.* Drain; transfer to serving dish and top with parsley. Add toasted slivered almonds, if desired. Serve immediately. Makes 6 servings.

Original Caesar Salad

Garlic Olive Oil
Caesar Croutons
3 medium heads romaine, chilled
    and broken into 2- or 3-inch
    pieces (16 cups)
2 to 3 tablespoons wine vinegar
1 lemon, halved
2 1-minute coddled eggs*
    Dash Worcestershire sauce
    Whole black pepper
⅓ cup grated Parmesan cheese
    Rolled anchovy fillets
    (optional)

One or more days before serving prepare Garlic Olive Oil. Several hours before serving prepare Caesar Croutons. Chill salad bowl and dinner plates.

At serving time place romaine in *chilled* salad bowl. Drizzle with about ⅓ cup Garlic Olive Oil; drizzle with vinegar. Squeeze lemon over; break in eggs. Add Worcestershire; sprinkle with salt. Generously grind pepper over; sprinkle with cheese. Toss lightly till dressing is well combined and romaine is coated. Add Caesar Croutons; toss once or twice. Serve immediately on *chilled* dinner plates. Garnish with anchovies, if desired. Makes 6 to 8 servings.

Garlic Olive Oil: Slice 6 cloves garlic lengthwise into quarters; combine with 1 cup olive *or* salad oil. Store in covered jar in refrigerator. Remove garlic before using oil.

Caesar Croutons: Cut 3 slices bread into ½-inch cubes. Spread out on baking sheet; pour a little Garlic Olive Oil over bread. Heat at 250° about 1 hour. Sprinkle with grated Parmesan cheese. Store croutons in covered jar in refrigerator.

*To coddle eggs, place eggs in shell in boiling water; remove from heat and let stand 1 minute. Cool slightly.

Mushrooms

Selecting: Since mushrooms are cultivated indoors under controlled conditions, they are always in season. Freshness and shape come first when selecting mushrooms. Look for caps that are closed around the stem. Wilting and wide-open caps are signs of age. Color should be uniform, but depends on the mushroom variety; white, off-white, and tan are the most common. Size alone does not indicate tenderness; popular varieties range in diameter from ¾ inch to 3 inches. Highly perishable, mushrooms should be purchased for immediate use. If not used at once, refrigerate in the original covered carton or in a plastic bag up to two days.

Preparing: Rinse gently in cold water; pat dry. Slice through cap and stem, chop, or use whole.

Serving: Raw mushrooms are tasty in salads. Cooked mushrooms add flavor to soups, casseroles, and other main dishes. Serve sautéed mushrooms as a vegetable or as a topper for steaks or burgers. To sauté, sprinkle 2 cups sliced fresh mushrooms with 1 teaspoon all-purpose flour. Cover; cook slowly in 1 tablespoon butter; stir occasionally. Season to taste.

Mushroom-Sauced Eggs

2 **cups fresh mushrooms (5 ounces)**
4 **teaspoons all-purpose flour**
2 **tablespoons butter *or* margarine**
¾ **cup milk**
1½ **teaspoons Worcestershire sauce**
¾ **teaspoon dry mustard**
½ **teaspoon paprika**
¼ **teaspoon salt**
Dash pepper
Poached Eggs
2 **English muffins, split and toasted**

Chop mushrooms; sprinkle with flour. In 1½-quart saucepan cook mushrooms in butter, covered, for 5 minutes, stirring occasionally. Stir in next 6 ingredients. Cook, uncovered, stirring constantly, till thickened and bubbly; boil for 1 minute. Cover; keep warm. Prepare Poached Eggs. Place Poached Eggs on muffin halves. Spoon sauce over. Serves 4.

Poached Eggs: Add water to a medium skillet to depth of 2 inches; bring just to boiling. Reduce heat. Using 4 eggs, break eggs, one at a time, into a saucer. Slide egg into simmering water. Working quickly, repeat with remaining 3 eggs. Simmer, uncovered, till whites are firm, 3 to 5 minutes. Remove with slotted spoon.

Microwave cooking directions: Chop mushrooms; sprinkle with flour. In a 1-quart nonmetal casserole combine mushrooms and butter. Cook in countertop microwave oven about 3½ minutes, stirring after 2 minutes. Stir in next 6 ingredients. Micro-cook till thickened and bubbly, about 3 minutes, stirring every 30 seconds. Cover; keep warm. Prepare Poached Eggs and serve as above.

Pickled Mushrooms

1 **small onion, thinly sliced**
   and separated into rings
⅓ **cup dry white wine**
⅓ **cup white wine vinegar**
⅓ **cup salad oil**
2 **tablespoons snipped parsley**
1 **small clove garlic, minced**
1 **bay leaf**
1 **teaspoon salt**
¼ **teaspoon dried thyme, crushed**
   Dash freshly ground pepper
4 **cups small fresh whole**
   mushrooms (10 ounces) *or* **2**
   8-ounce cans whole
   mushrooms, drained

In saucepan combine onion, wine, vinegar, salad oil, parsley, garlic, bay leaf, salt, thyme, and pepper; bring to boiling. Add fresh or canned mushrooms and return to boiling. Simmer, uncovered, for 10 minutes. Cool. Transfer to covered container; chill at least 24 hours before serving. Store in refrigerator up to 2 weeks. Makes 2 cups.

Cream of Mushroom Soup

1 **cup sliced fresh mushrooms**
2 **tablespoons chopped onion**
2 **tablespoons butter** *or*
   margarine
2 **tablespoons all-purpose flour**
2 **cups chicken broth**
1 **cup whipping cream**
¼ **teaspoon salt**
¼ **teaspoon ground nutmeg**
⅛ **teaspoon white pepper**

Cook mushrooms and onion in butter or margarine till tender but not brown, about 5 minutes. Blend in flour; add chicken broth. Cook, stirring constantly, till slightly thickened and bubbly. Stir in whipping cream, salt, nutmeg, and white pepper. Heat through. Makes 4 to 6 servings.

Dill-Stuffed Mushrooms

24 **large fresh mushrooms**
 2 **tablespoons sliced green onion**
   with tops
 2 **tablespoons butter** *or*
   margarine
¼ **cup fine dry bread crumbs**
½ **teaspoon dried dillweed**
⅛ **teaspoon salt**
⅛ **teaspoon Worcestershire sauce**

Remove stems from mushrooms; chop stems. Cook stems and onion in butter till tender. Remove from heat. Stir in bread crumbs, dillweed, salt, and Worcestershire; fill mushroom crowns with bread crumb mixture. Bake on greased baking sheet at 425° for 6 to 8 minutes. Makes 24.

Mushroom Cocktail

⅓ **cup catsup**
 1 **tablespoon vinegar**
¼ **teaspoon prepared horseradish**
   Lettuce leaves
1½ **cups shredded lettuce**
12 **medium fresh mushrooms, sliced**

In small bowl combine catsup, vinegar, and horseradish. Chill. Line 6 sherbets with lettuce leaves; top with shredded lettuce. Arrange about ¼ cup sliced mushrooms atop each. Chill. Just before serving, drizzle each with about 1 tablespoon catsup mixture. Makes 6 servings.

Okra

Selecting: *This podded vegetable, a standby with Southern cooks as an ingredient in Creole dishes, is now becoming available everywhere. Peak quantities of okra come to market from June to September. Choose fresh, tender pods, and avoid those that look dull, dry, or shriveled. Both smooth and ridged okra is grown. Depending on the variety, sizes range from thick 3-inch to slender 7-inch pods. Coloring, from deep to light green, also varies with type of okra. Store in a plastic bag in the refrigerator crisper up to two weeks.*

Preparing: *Wash okra pods and cut off stems.*

Cooking: *In covered pan cook in small amount of boiling salted water till tender, 8 to 15 minutes. (Do not use iron, copper, brass, or tin utensils; okra discolors and is unappetizing.)*

Serving: *Dip sliced okra in cornmeal and pan-fry quickly. Sliced into stews and gumbos, okra lends both flavor and thickening.*

Southern Vegetable Medley

4 ounces salt pork
4 fresh ears of corn
½ pound okra, sliced (2 cups)
1 cup water
½ cup chopped onion
1 to 2 teaspoons chili powder
1 teaspoon instant beef bouillon
    granules
4 medium tomatoes, peeled and
    cut up

Rinse and chop salt pork. In 10-inch skillet cook salt pork till crisp. Cut corn from cobs. Add corn, fresh okra, water, onion, chili powder, and beef bouillon granules to salt pork in skillet. Bring to boiling; reduce heat. Cover and simmer 20 minutes. Add tomatoes; cover and simmer 10 minutes longer. Makes 8 servings.

Garlic Okra Pickles

3 pounds okra
3 cups water
1 cup white vinegar
¼ cup pickling salt
2 cloves garlic, minced

Pack whole fresh okra into hot, clean pint jars. Combine remaining ingredients; bring to boiling. Slowly pour boiling liquid into jars, leaving ½-inch headspace. Prepare lids according to manufacturer's directions. Wipe jar rim. Adjust lid. Process jars in boiling water bath for 5 minutes (start timing when water returns to boil). Makes 4 pints.

You don't have to live on the Gulf Coast to enjoy flavorful *Creole Gumbo.* This savory
version of seafood-okra stew is made with fresh or frozen okra and canned shrimp and crab meat.

Brunswick Stew

1 6-pound ready-to-cook
  stewing chicken
3 potatoes, peeled and cubed
2 large onions, sliced
2 cups sliced okra *or* 1 10-ounce
  package frozen cut okra
2 17-ounce cans whole kernel
  corn, drained
1 28-ounce can tomatoes
1 10-ounce package frozen lima
  beans
1 tablespoon sugar

Cut up stewing chicken. In large kettle or Dutch oven combine cut-up chicken and 6 cups water. Bring to boiling. Reduce heat and simmer till chicken is tender, 1½ to 2 hours. Remove chicken from broth; cool chicken and broth. Remove meat from bones. Cube meat; discard skin and bones. Skim fat from broth. Add cubed chicken to broth. Add potatoes, sliced onions, fresh or frozen okra, corn, tomatoes, lima beans, sugar, 4 teaspoons salt, and ¼ teaspoon pepper. Cover and simmer till vegetables are tender and flavors are blended, about 30 minutes. Makes 16 servings.

Meatball-Okra Stew

1 slightly beaten egg
¼ cup fine dry bread crumbs
¼ cup milk
½ teaspoon dried oregano,
  crushed
1 pound lean ground beef
4 teaspoons instant beef
  bouillon granules
1 tablespoon Worcestershire
  sauce
1 clove garlic, minced
1 teaspoon chili powder
1½ cups coarsely chopped onion
4 potatoes, peeled and chopped
10 ounces okra, cut up (2 cups)

In mixing bowl combine egg, bread crumbs, milk, oregano, ½ teaspoon salt, and ⅛ teaspoon pepper. Add ground beef and mix well. Shape mixture into 48 small meatballs. In large saucepan combine bouillon granules, Worcestershire, garlic, chili powder, 4 cups water, and ⅛ teaspoon pepper. Bring to boiling; add meatballs and onion. Cover and simmer 20 minutes. Add potatoes and okra; simmer till vegetables are tender, about 10 minutes longer. Makes 8 servings.

Creole Gumbo

½ cup chopped onion
1 clove garlic, minced
3 tablespoons butter
3 tablespoons all-purpose flour
1 16-ounce can tomatoes, cut up
½ cup chopped green pepper
2 bay leaves
1 teaspoon dried oregano,
  crushed
1 teaspoon dried thyme, crushed
¼ to ½ teaspoon bottled hot
  pepper sauce
10 ounces okra, cut up
  (2 cups), *or* 1 10-ounce
  package frozen cut okra
2 4½-ounce cans shrimp, drained
1 7½-ounce can crab meat,
  drained, flaked, and
  cartilage removed
  Hot cooked rice

In large saucepan cook onion and garlic in butter till onion is tender but not brown. Blend in flour. Cook, stirring constantly, till flour is golden brown. Stir in undrained tomatoes, green pepper, bay leaves, oregano, thyme, hot pepper sauce, 1½ cups water, and ½ teaspoon salt. Bring to boiling; reduce heat and simmer, covered, 20 minutes.

Remove bay leaves. Stir in the fresh or frozen okra; bring mixture to boiling. Simmer for 5 minutes. Cut up any large shrimp. Stir shrimp and crab meat into okra mixture and heat through, about 5 minutes. Serve the gumbo mixture over hot cooked rice in soup plates. (Traditionally, hot cooked rice is mounded in a heated soup plate and the gumbo spooned around it.) Makes 6 servings.

Onions, Leeks & Shallots

Selecting: Most varieties of onions are in good supply year-round. Select dry onions or shallots for their bright, thin skins; the bulbs should be firm, thin-necked, and free of blemishes. Store in a cool, dry, well-ventilated area. Green onions and leeks should have firm, white bulbs and bright green tops. Refrigerate in a plastic bag up to a week.

Preparing: Peel dry onions and shallots. Leave small boiling onions whole, but cut off ends. Wash green onions and leeks to remove sand. Trim roots and tops, but save 2 to 3 inches of the green tops.

Cooking: In a covered pan cook quartered or small whole onions in boiling salted water till tender, 25 to 30 minutes; cook leeks 15 minutes.

Serving: Onions add flavor to many dishes. Shallots are usually chopped and used as a seasoning. Leeks and small onions are often served in cream sauce. Add raw mild onions and leeks to salads.

French Onion Soup

1½ pounds onions, thinly sliced
   (6 cups)
¼ cup butter *or* margarine
3 10½-ounce cans condensed
   beef broth
1 teaspoon Worcestershire sauce
¼ teaspoon salt
6 to 8 slices French bread *or*
   hard rolls, toasted
   Grated Parmesan cheese

In a covered 3-quart saucepan cook sliced onions in butter till tender, about 20 minutes. Add beef broth, Worcestershire sauce, salt, and dash pepper. Bring to boiling.

Sprinkle toast slices with grated Parmesan cheese; place under broiler till cheese is lightly browned. Ladle soup into bowls and float toast slices atop. (Or, place a toast slice on soup in each broiler-proof soup bowl; sprinkle with Parmesan cheese and place bowl under broiler till cheese is lightly browned.) Makes 6 to 8 servings.

Creamed Onions

3 medium onions
3 tablespoons butter
2 tablespoons all-purpose flour
¼ teaspoon salt
   Dash white pepper
1⅓ cups milk
1 cup shredded Muenster cheese

Cut onions into small wedges. In covered pan cook onions in boiling salted water till nearly tender, 8 to 10 minutes. Drain well. In saucepan melt butter; blend in flour, salt, and white pepper. Add milk all at once; cook and stir till thickened and bubbly. Add shredded Muenster cheese; stir till melted. Stir in drained onions; heat through. Garnish with parsley, if desired. Makes 6 to 8 servings.

There's no better way to start a meal than with steaming bowls of *French Onion Soup.*
Use canned beef broth to shortcut preparation without sacrificing any of the classic flavor.

Perfect French-Fried Onions

⅔ cup milk
1 egg
3 Bermuda *or* mild white onions, sliced ¼ inch thick and separated into rings
1 cup all-purpose flour
Fat for deep-fat frying

In bowl combine milk and egg; beat well. Pour into shallow pan. Drop a few onion rings into pan. With fingers, turn rings till each is well coated. Lift out; drain off excess mixture. Then, drop rings into pan of flour, a few at a time; turn to coat well. Shake to remove excess flour.

Fill French-frying basket only ¼ full of onions. Set basket into deep hot fat (375°). Stir once with a fork to separate. When onion rings are golden brown, remove from fat and drain on paper toweling. To keep onions crisp, don't salt until just before serving. Makes 8 servings.

Oxtail-Leek Stew (pictured on pages 4-5)

⅓ cup all-purpose flour
5 pounds oxtails, disjointed
¼ cup shortening
1 cup chopped onion
¾ cup chopped peeled tomato
1 large carrot, quartered
1 medium turnip, peeled and quartered
2 cloves garlic, minced
Few sprigs parsley
1 bay leaf
2 10½-ounce cans condensed beef broth
1¼ cups port
1 cup water
1½ cups sliced carrots
2 cups sliced leeks

Combine flour, 2 teaspoons salt, and dash pepper. Coat oxtails with flour mixture. In large Dutch oven brown oxtails in hot shortening, turning often; drain off fat. Add onion, tomato, the quartered carrot, turnip, garlic, parsley, and bay leaf. Stir in broth, ¼ *cup* of the port, and water. Bring to boiling; reduce heat. Cover and simmer till oxtails are almost tender, about 1½ hours.

Remove and discard the cooked carrot, turnip, parsley, and bay leaf. Skim off fat. Return mixture to boiling; reduce heat and stir in the remaining 1 cup port. Add 1 teaspoon salt and dash pepper. Simmer, covered, for 30 minutes. Add sliced carrots; simmer 10 minutes longer. Add leeks; simmer till vegetables are just tender, 10 to 15 minutes longer. If desired, serve with boiled potatoes and sprinkle with snipped parsley. Makes 6 to 8 servings.

Shallot Soufflé with Mushroom Sauce

1 tablespoon butter *or* margarine
2 tablespoons grated Parmesan cheese
¼ cup finely chopped shallots
¼ cup butter *or* margarine
¼ cup all-purpose flour
1 cup milk
½ teaspoon salt
2 dashes bottled hot pepper sauce
1 cup shredded Cheddar cheese (4 ounces)
4 egg yolks
4 stiffly beaten egg whites
Mushroom Sauce

Spread the 1 tablespoon butter over bottom and sides of a 1½-quart soufflé dish. Sprinkle with the Parmesan cheese.

In saucepan cook shallots in the ¼ cup butter till tender but not brown; blend in flour. Add milk, salt, and hot pepper sauce; cook and stir till thickened and bubbly. Remove from heat. Stir in Cheddar cheese till melted.

Beat egg yolks on high speed of electric mixer till thick and lemon-colored, about 5 minutes. Slowly add cheese mixture, stirring constantly; cool slightly. Slowly pour yolk mixture over stiffly beaten egg whites; fold together well. Turn into prepared dish. Bake at 300° till knife inserted just off-center comes out clean, about 1¼ hours. Serve immediately with Mushroom Sauce. Makes 6 servings.

Mushroom Sauce: In medium skillet cook 2 cups sliced fresh mushrooms (5 ounces) and 2 tablespoons finely chopped shallots in 3 tablespoons butter till tender, 5 to 7 minutes. Add 4 teaspoons all-purpose flour, ⅛ teaspoon salt, and dash pepper; stir till smooth. Add ½ cup whipping cream all at once. Cook and stir till thickened and bubbly.

Oriental Vegetables

Selecting: *Vegetables commonly used in Oriental cooking are diverse. Bean sprouts have a delicate flavor and crunchy texture; look for crisp, plump, white sprouts. Pea pods (also known as sugar peas and snow peas) should be bright green and crisp. Fresh gnarled gingerroot has an ivory interior with a pungent, spicy flavor; select fresh-looking, firm roots. Look for Chinese cabbage, also known as celery cabbage, with a firm, compact head and fresh, crinkled, light green leaves. Bok choy has long white stems and large dark green leaves; look for leaves that are fresh and shiny.*

Preparing: *For bean sprouts, remove roots, if desired; rinse sprouts. Wash pea pods; remove tips and strings (do not shell). Peel gingerroot, if desired; grate, slice, or chop. For Chinese cabbage or bok choy, discard any tough outer stalks and rinse well.*

Serving: *Serve raw Oriental vegetables in salads. Or cook, but very briefly so crispness is retained.*

Oriental Garden Toss

6 ounces pea pods *or*
 1 6-ounce package frozen
 pea pods, thawed
½ cup salad oil
⅓ cup vinegar
2 tablespoons sugar
1 tablespoon soy sauce
¼ teaspoon ground ginger
½ teaspoon salt
⅛ teaspoon freshly ground pepper
3 cups sliced bok choy
3 cups torn leaf lettuce
1 cup bean sprouts
2 tablespoons chopped pimiento

Remove tips and strings from fresh pea pods. In covered pan cook fresh or frozen pea pods in 2 cups boiling salted water for 1 minute; drain well.

In screw-top jar combine oil, vinegar, sugar, soy sauce, gingerroot or ginger, salt, and pepper; cover and shake vigorously. Pour mixture over pea pods; cover and marinate in refrigerator for 1 to 1½ hours.

At serving time combine bok choy, leaf lettuce, bean sprouts, and pimiento in large salad bowl. Add pea pods and marinade. Toss to coat vegetables. Makes 6 to 8 servings.

Sukiyaki

½ pound beef tenderloin
6 to 8 ounces bean curd (tofu)
1 cup bean sprouts *or* ½ of a
    16-ounce can bean sprouts
2 ounces fresh water chestnuts,
    peeled, *or* ½ of an 8-ounce
    can water chestnuts, drained
½ of a 5-ounce can bamboo shoots
1 tablespoon cooking oil
1 tablespoon sugar
½ teaspoon instant beef bouillon
    granules
¼ cup boiling water
3 tablespoons soy sauce
1 cup bias-sliced green onion
    with tops
½ cup bias-sliced celery
3 cups torn bok choy *or* small
    spinach leaves
½ cup thinly sliced fresh
    mushrooms
    Hot cooked rice

Partially freeze beef. Slice beef very thinly across the grain. Cube bean curd. Drain canned bean sprouts. Thinly slice fresh or canned water chestnuts. Drain bamboo shoots.

Preheat a large skillet or wok; add oil. Add beef slices; cook quickly, turning meat over and over, just till browned, 1 to 2 minutes. Sprinkle with sugar. Dissolve bouillon granules in boiling water; add soy sauce. Pour over meat. Remove meat from skillet with a slotted spoon. Let soy mixture bubble. Add onion and celery. Continue cooking and toss-stirring over high heat about 1 minute. Add bean curd, bean sprouts, water chestnuts, bamboo shoots, bok choy or spinach, and mushrooms. Return meat to pan. Cook and stir just till heated through. Serve with hot cooked rice. Pass soy sauce, if desired. Makes 2 or 3 servings.

Hot Firepot

1 2-ounce package *dried*
    mushrooms
1 pound beef flank steak
½ cup sesame oil *or* cooking oil
¼ teaspoon garlic salt
1 pound fresh *or* frozen shrimp,
    shelled and deveined
½ pound fresh *or* frozen white
    fish
2 cups spinach
1 head Chinese cabbage
4 to 6 cups chicken broth
4 ounces fresh whole bamboo
    shoots, cut up, *or* 1 5-ounce
    can bamboo shoots, drained
    Hong Kong Dip
1 cup fine noodles

Soak mushrooms in water according to package directions. Partially freeze beef. Slice beef across the grain into ¼-inch-wide strips. Combine oil and garlic salt; marinate meat in oil mixture for a few hours. Drain well. Thaw shrimp, if frozen. Sprinkle shrimp with 1 teaspoon salt. Let stand 10 minutes; rinse. Thaw fish, if frozen. Cut fish into ½-inch cubes; sprinkle lightly with salt. Cut fresh spinach and Chinese cabbage into 2-inch-wide strips; halve strips crosswise.

Pour broth into firepot till about half full; heat to boiling according to firepot manufacturer's directions. (*Or*, pour broth into metal fondue pot till about half full; heat to boiling on range top. Transfer to fondue burner.) Arrange all of the meats and vegetables in Oriental cooking baskets, or spear with fondue forks; cook in hot broth till done. Serve with Hong Kong Dip. Drop noodles into the remaining boiling broth. Cook till tender but still firm. Ladle soup into bowls. Serves 6.

Hong Kong Dip: In small saucepan heat 1 cup sesame oil *or* cooking oil. Remove from heat. Stir in 2 tablespoons soy sauce and ¼ teaspoon bottled hot pepper sauce.

Buttered Pea Pods

12 ounces pea pods (4 cups)
    or 2 6-ounce packages
    frozen pea pods
½ teaspoon sugar
2 tablespoons butter

Remove tips and strings from fresh pea pods. In saucepan combine fresh or frozen pea pods, sugar, ½ cup water, and 1 teaspoon salt. Cover; bring to boiling. Boil 2 minutes; drain well. Heat and stir butter till light golden; toss with pea pods. Season with salt and pepper. Makes 6 to 8 servings.

Oriental vegetables contribute a variety of colors, flavors, and textures to Japanese *Sukiyaki*. It takes only a few minutes to cook, so cut up meat and vegetables before you begin.

Parsnips

Selecting: You'll find parsnips in the market all year, but they're most plentiful during the fall and winter months. Buy firm, well-shaped vegetables that are free of major blemishes. The best ones to buy are small to medium in size, as larger roots tend to be woody. Wrap parsnips tightly and store in the refrigerator crisper up to two weeks.

Preparing: Wash parsnips, then scrape or peel to remove outer skin. Leave whole or cut in slices, julienne strips, or halves.

Cooking: In covered pan cook parsnips in a small amount of boiling salted water till tender, 25 to 40 minutes for whole parsnips; 15 to 20 minutes for strips, halves, or slices. For a menu variation, arrange a few cut-up parsnips around a beef pot roast during the last 40 to 60 minutes of cooking; baste the vegetables frequently with pan juices.

Serving: Serve hot cooked parsnips with butter and sprinkle with a little sugar, if desired. Serve with a cream sauce or a glaze sprinkled with nutmeg, or mash as you would potatoes. Add rich flavor to soups and stews with a few cut-up parsnips, or deep-fat fry thin slices for a snack that resembles potato chips.

Whipped Parsnips and Sweet Potatoes (pictured on pages 4-5)

1 pound parsnips
1 pound sweet potatoes
2 tablespoons butter
½ teaspoon salt
¼ teaspoon ground allspice
Milk (optional)

Peel and slice parsnips and potatoes. In covered pan cook vegetables in a small amount of boiling salted water till tender, about 15 minutes; drain. In mixer bowl combine hot vegetables, butter, salt, and allspice. Beat till smooth; add milk, if needed, to make fluffy. If desired, top with sliced green onion with tops and more butter. Serves 4 to 6.

Hawaiian-Style Parsnips

2 pounds parsnips (10 medium)
2 tablespoons brown sugar
1 tablespoon cornstarch
1 8¼-ounce can crushed pineapple
½ teaspoon shredded orange peel
½ cup orange juice
2 tablespoons butter

Peel and slice parsnips. Cook as directed above; drain well. In large saucepan blend brown sugar, cornstarch, and ¾ teaspoon salt; stir in undrained pineapple, orange peel, and orange juice. Cook and stir till thickened and bubbly. Add butter; stir till melted. Add parsnips to sauce. Cover and simmer 5 minutes. Makes 6 to 8 servings.

Peas

Selecting: *The peak season for fresh peas is May through August; look for bright green, crisp, well-filled pods. Choose fresh black-eyed peas with crisp, full pods. Refrigerate peas in their pods and use as soon as possible. Store all dry peas in a cool, dry place.*

Preparing: *Shell fresh peas; wash. Rinse dry peas. Split peas do not need to be soaked. Place dry whole or black-eyed peas in kettle with about 4 times as much water as peas. Cover pan; soak overnight. (Or, bring to boil; simmer 2 minutes. Remove from heat. Cover; soak 1 hour.) Do not drain.*

Cooking: *In covered pan cook fresh peas in small amount of boiling salted water till just tender, 10 to 12 minutes; cook fresh black-eyed peas till tender. In covered pan cook unsoaked split peas in about 4 times as much water as vegetables for 1½ to 2 hours. Cook soaked dry whole or black-eyed peas for 1 to 1½ hours.*

Serving: *Offer buttered peas with an herb for a fresh-tasting dish; try basil, marjoram, or sage. Creamed peas and new potatoes is a popular combination. Dry peas or black-eyed peas are tasty additions to soup.*

Deluxe Peas and Mushrooms

2 cups shelled peas *or* 1
   10-ounce package frozen peas
1 cup sliced fresh mushrooms
¼ cup chopped onion
2 tablespoons butter
1 teaspoon sugar
1 tablespoon chopped pimiento

Cook fresh peas as directed above. (Or, cook frozen peas according to package directions.) Drain well

Cook mushrooms and onion in butter till tender. Stir in sugar, ½ teaspoon salt, and dash pepper. Add cooked peas and pimiento. Cover and heat through. Makes 4 servings.

Oven-Style Peas

1 20-ounce package frozen peas
1 2½-ounce jar sliced mushrooms, drained
¼ cup chopped onion
2 tablespoons butter
¼ teaspoon dried savory, crushed

In a 1½-quart casserole combine frozen peas, mushrooms, onion, butter, savory, 1 tablespoon water, ¼ teaspoon salt, and dash pepper. Cover and bake at 350° till peas are tender, 45 to 50 minutes, stirring after 20 minutes. Serves 8.

Pea-Cheese Salad

2 cups shelled peas *or*
    1 10-ounce package frozen
    peas *or* 1 17-ounce can peas
1 cup cubed Cheddar cheese
2 hard-cooked eggs, chopped
¼ cup chopped celery
2 tablespoons chopped onion
2 tablespoons chopped pimiento
⅓ cup mayonnaise *or* salad
    dressing
½ teaspoon salt
¼ teaspoon bottled hot pepper
    sauce
⅛ teaspoon pepper
6 medium tomatoes
    Lettuce leaves

Cook fresh peas as directed on page 63. (Or, cook frozen peas according to package directions.) Thoroughly drain the cooked or canned peas. Cool cooked peas.

In large bowl combine peas, cheese cubes, hard-cooked eggs, celery, onion, and pimiento. Combine mayonnaise or salad dressing, salt, hot pepper sauce, and pepper. Add to pea mixture; toss to combine. Cover and refrigerate several hours or overnight. Stir mixture well.

Cut each tomato into 8 wedges, cutting to, but not through, bottom of tomato. On salad plates, place tomatoes atop lettuce leaves; fill with pea mixture. Makes 6 servings.

Creamed Peas and Onions

2 cups shelled peas *or* 1
    10-ounce package frozen peas
1 cup whole pearl onions *or*
    frozen small whole onions
1 tablespoon butter *or* margarine
1 tablespoon all-purpose flour
½ teaspoon salt
    Dash white pepper
1 cup milk
    Grated Parmesan cheese

In a covered saucepan cook fresh peas and pearl or frozen onions in boiling salted water till tender, about 10 minutes. (If using frozen peas, add to onions only during the last 5 minutes.) Drain peas and onions well.

Meanwhile, melt butter or margarine in saucepan over low heat. Blend in flour, salt, and white pepper. Add milk all at once; cook and stir till thickened and bubbly. Pour over hot vegetables; stir to coat vegetables. Serve in sauce dishes. Pass Parmesan cheese. Makes 4 servings.

Springtime Peas

3 to 6 lettuce leaves
2 cups shelled peas *or* 1
    10-ounce package frozen peas
¼ cup sliced green onion
    with tops
1 teaspoon sugar
    Dash dried thyme, crushed
1 tablespoon butter *or* margarine

Moisten lettuce leaves, leaving a few drops of water clinging. Line bottom of a 10-inch skillet with lettuce leaves. Top with fresh or frozen peas and green onion. Sprinkle with sugar, thyme, ½ teaspoon salt, and dash pepper. Cover tightly and cook over low heat till peas are tender, 18 to 20 minutes. Remove lettuce. Drain peas well; dot with butter or margarine. Makes 4 servings.

Creole Peas

2 cups shelled peas *or*
    1 10-ounce package frozen
    peas *or* 1 17-ounce can peas
¼ cup chopped onion
¼ cup chopped green pepper
2 tablespoons butter
1 8-ounce can tomatoes, cut up
2 teaspoons cornstarch

Cook fresh peas as directed on page 63. (Or, cook frozen peas according to package directions.) Thoroughly drain the cooked or canned peas. In saucepan cook onion and green pepper in butter till tender but not brown. Drain tomatoes, reserving liquid. Add tomatoes to cooked onion. Stir in peas, ½ teaspoon salt, and dash pepper. Blend tomato liquid into cornstarch; stir into pea mixture. Cook and stir till thickened and bubbly. Makes 4 servings.

A seasonal treat that's well worth waiting for is a dish of fresh green peas. You know how delicious they are in traditional *Creamed Peas and Onions;* now try them in *Pea-Cheese Salad.*

Minted New Peas

½ cup chopped green onion
    with tops
3 tablespoons butter
2 cups shelled peas *or* 1
    10-ounce package frozen peas
1 tablespoon finely chopped
    fresh mint leaves
1 teaspoon sugar
1 teaspoon lemon juice
¼ teaspoon salt
¼ teaspoon dried rosemary,
    crushed

Cook green onion in butter till tender. Add fresh or frozen peas, chopped fresh mint, sugar, lemon juice, salt, rosemary, and 2 tablespoons water. Cover and cook till peas are just tender, 10 to 12 minutes, adding a little more water as necessary. Garnish with lemon twist and fresh mint leaves, if desired. Makes 4 servings.

French-Canadian Split Pea Soup

1 pound dry green split peas
1 meaty ham bone
1 cup chopped onion
1 teaspoon instant chicken
    bouillon granules
½ teaspoon salt
¼ teaspoon pepper
1 cup sliced carrot
1 cup chopped celery
2 slices bacon
½ cup light cream
2 tablespoons butter

Rinse peas. In kettle mix peas, ham bone, onion, bouillon granules, salt, pepper, and 8 cups water. Bring to boiling. Reduce heat; cover and simmer 1½ hours, stirring often.

Remove ham bone; chop meat. Return meat to soup; add carrot and celery. Simmer 30 minutes. Cook bacon till crisp; drain and crumble. Stir bacon, light cream, and butter into soup; heat through. Makes 8 servings.

Ham Hocks and Black-Eyed Peas

3 cups dry black-eyed peas
3 pounds ham hocks
1¼ cups chopped onion
1 cup chopped celery
1 bay leaf
1 teaspoon salt
⅛ teaspoon cayenne
10 ounces okra, cut up (2 cups),
    or 1 10-ounce package
    frozen cut okra

Place dry peas in a 6-quart kettle or Dutch oven and add 12 cups water. Soak as directed on page 63. *Do not drain.*

Stir in ham hocks, onion, celery, bay leaf, salt, and cayenne. Bring to boiling. Reduce heat; cover and simmer till ham hocks are tender and peas are done, about 1½ hours. Stir in fresh or frozen okra; cook till okra is very tender, 10 to 15 minutes. Remove bay leaf. Season to taste with salt and pepper. Makes 6 servings.

Hoppin' John

1 cup dry black-eyed peas
8 cups water
6 slices bacon
¾ cup chopped onion
1 clove garlic, minced
1 cup regular rice
2 teaspoons salt
¼ teaspoon pepper

Soak dry peas, using 8 cups water, as directed on page 63. Drain mixture, reserving 6 *cups* of the liquid.

In heavy 3-quart saucepan cook bacon, onion, and garlic till bacon is crisp and onion is tender. Remove bacon; drain. Crumble and set aside. Stir peas, rice, salt, pepper, and reserved liquid into onion mixture. Bring to boiling; reduce heat. Cover; simmer 1 hour, stirring occasionally. To serve, stir in crumbled bacon. Makes 8 servings.

Peppers

Selecting: This family ranges from the common sweet bell pepper to the extremely hot chili pepper. Although usually sold while still green, bell peppers will turn bright red if allowed to mature fully. Look for well-shaped, firm, unblemished vegetables that have a bright color. Store in refrigerator crisper, but plan to use within a few days.

Preparing: Remove the stems, seeds, and inner membranes of bell peppers before using. Fresh or dried hot peppers must be handled very carefully because the oil from the peppers can burn your eyes or skin. In fact, it's a good idea to wear rubber gloves and hold the peppers under cold running water during preparation. For hot peppers, remove the stems, seeds (these are very hot), and inner membranes.

Cooking: Precook bell peppers that are to be stuffed by immersing in boiling salted water for 3 to 5 minutes. Cook hot peppers as directed in specific recipes.

Serving: Green peppers are flavorful additions to salads, soups, dips, and casseroles. Hot peppers are particularly popular in Southwestern and Mexican dishes.

Garden-Stuffed Peppers (pictured on page 68)

4 large green peppers
3 or 4 fresh ears of corn *or* 1 12-ounce can whole kernel corn, drained
¼ cup chopped onion
2 tablespoons butter *or* margarine
1 cup shelled baby lima beans, cooked and drained, *or* 1 10-ounce package frozen baby lima beans, cooked and drained
1 large tomato, chopped
½ teaspoon dried rosemary, crushed
¾ cup soft bread crumbs (1 slice) (optional)
1 tablespoon butter *or* margarine, melted (optional)

Remove tops from green peppers. Cut peppers in half longthwice and remove seeds. Cook peppers in boiling salted water for 3 to 5 minutes; invert to drain. If using fresh corn, cut off tips of corn kernels. Carefully scrape cobs with dull edge of knife; measure 1½ cups corn. In covered pan cook fresh corn in a small amount of boiling salted water till done, 12 to 15 minutes; drain.

Cook onion in the 2 tablespoons butter or margarine till tender but not brown. Stir in cooked or canned corn, lima beans, chopped tomato, and rosemary.

Season green pepper shells with salt and pepper. Fill peppers with vegetable mixture. If desired, toss soft bread crumbs with the melted butter or margarine; sprinkle atop peppers. Place in a 13x9x2-inch baking dish. Bake at 350° for 30 minutes. Makes 8 servings.

Garden-Stuffed Peppers are heaped with a corn-tomato-lima bean filling (see recipe, page 67). During the off-season, substitute canned corn and frozen limas for their fresh counterparts.

Chilies Rellenos Bake

2 4-ounce cans green chili
    peppers (6 chili peppers)
6 ounces Monterey Jack cheese
4 beaten eggs
⅓ cup milk
½ cup all-purpose flour
½ teaspoon baking powder
½ teaspoon salt
½ cup shredded Cheddar cheese

Drain peppers; halve lengthwise and remove seeds. Cut Monterey Jack cheese into strips to fit inside peppers. Wrap each pepper around a strip of Monterey Jack cheese; place in a greased 10x6x2-inch baking dish. Combine eggs and milk; beat in flour, baking powder, and salt till smooth. Pour over peppers. Sprinkle Cheddar cheese atop. Bake at 350° till golden, about 30 minutes. Makes 6 servings.

Red Pepper Relish

24 sweet red peppers, halved and
    seeded
7 medium onions, halved
3 cups sugar
3 cups vinegar
2 tablespoons salt

Thinly slice peppers and onions, or use coarse blade to grind peppers and onions. Reserve vegetable juices. In 4- to 6-quart kettle or Dutch oven combine reserved juices, peppers, onions, sugar, vinegar, and salt. Bring to boiling. Reduce heat; simmer 30 minutes. Pour into hot, clean half-pint jars, leaving ½-inch headspace. Prepare lids according to manufacturer's directions. Wipe jar rim. Adjust lid on jar. Process in boiling water bath 15 minutes (start timing as soon as jars are placed in water). Makes 10 half-pints.

Beef in Pepper Cups

6 medium green peppers
1 pound ground beef
½ cup chopped onion
¾ teaspoon salt
    Dash pepper
1 16-ounce can tomatoes, cut up
½ cup regular rice
½ cup water
1 teaspoon Worcestershire sauce
½ teaspoon chili powder
1 cup shredded sharp American
    cheese (4 ounces)

Remove tops and seeds from green peppers; chop enough of the tops to make ¼ cup. Cook whole green peppers in boiling salted water for 3 to 5 minutes; invert to drain. Sprinkle insides of peppers lightly with salt. In skillet cook beef, onion, and the ¼ cup chopped green pepper till meat is brown and vegetables are tender. Drain off excess fat. Season with the ¾ teaspoon salt and pepper. Add tomatoes, uncooked rice, water, Worcestershire, and chili powder. Cover and simmer till rice is tender, 15 to 20 minutes. Stir in *half* the cheese. Stuff peppers with meat mixture. Bake in 12x7½x2-inch baking dish at 350° for 25 to 30 minutes. Sprinkle with remaining cheese; return to oven till cheese melts, 2 to 3 minutes longer. Makes 6 servings.

Hot Pickled Peppers

1 pound red, green, or yellow
    hot peppers (8 cups)
4 heads fresh dill or 2 table-
    spoons dillseed (optional)
3 cups water
1 cup white vinegar
2 tablespoons pickling salt
1 tablespoon sugar
2 cloves garlic, minced
¼ teaspoon crushed dried red
    pepper

Make 2 small slits in each hot pepper (wear rubber gloves to prevent burning hands). Pack peppers into hot, clean pint jars, leaving ½-inch headspace. If desired, place *1 head* of the fresh dill or *1½ teaspoons* of the dillseed in *each* jar. In saucepan combine water, white vinegar, pickling salt, sugar, garlic, and crushed red pepper; bring to boiling. Pour hot pickling liquid over peppers, leaving ½-inch headspace. Prepare lids according to manufacturer's directions. Wipe jar rim. Adjust lid on jar. Process jars in boiling water bath for 10 minutes (start timing when water returns to boiling). Makes 4 pints.

Potatoes

Selecting: Potato varieties range in shape from oblong to round, and in skin color from creamy white to red and russet brown. Although there are some all-purpose varieties, many are best suited to a specific use. In general, round potatoes have firm, waxy interiors that are best for boiling. Long, oval potatoes usually have mealy interiors and are best for baking, frying, or mashing. New potatoes are simply tiny, immature potatoes. Choose firm, smooth potatoes with shallow eyes. Avoid cut, sprouted, or blemished vegetables and those with patches of green on the skin. Store potatoes in a cool (about 55°), dark place.

Preparing: Use a knife or vegetable peeler to peel potatoes. If baking or cooking potatoes with the skins on, scrub thoroughly with a vegetable brush and remove any sprouts and green areas. After cooking, the skins peel off easily. Be sure to prick the potato skins before baking.

Cooking: Baking and boiling are the most common ways to cook potatoes. Bake potatoes at 425° for 40 to 60 minutes. Bake foil-wrapped potatoes at 350° till done, about 1½ hours.

In covered pan cook potatoes in boiling salted water till tender. Allow 25 to 40 minutes for whole potatoes, 20 to 25 minutes for quartered potatoes, 12 to 15 minutes for tiny new potatoes, and 10 to 15 minutes for cubed potatoes.

Hashed Brown Omelet

3 medium potatoes*
4 slices bacon
¼ cup chopped onion
¼ cup chopped green pepper
½ teaspoon salt
4 beaten eggs
¼ cup milk
¼ teaspoon salt
¼ teaspoon dried thyme, crushed
   Dash pepper
1 cup shredded Swiss cheese
   (4 ounces)

In covered pan cook whole potatoes in enough boiling salted water to cover till almost tender, 20 to 25 minutes; drain and chill. Peel potatoes; shred to make 3 cups. *(Or, substitute cooked packaged hashed brown potatoes.)

In 10-inch skillet cook bacon till crisp; drain, reserving 2 tablespoons drippings in skillet. Crumble bacon and set aside. Combine potatoes, onion, green pepper, and the ½ teaspoon salt; pat into skillet. Cook over low heat till underside is crisp and brown, about 20 minutes. Combine eggs, milk, the ¼ teaspoon salt, thyme, and pepper. Stir in bacon and cheese; pour over potatoes. Cover; cook over low heat till surface is set but still shiny, 8 to 10 minutes. Loosen edges of omelet; cut in wedges. Makes 4 servings.

Fresh Fries with Onion

4 cups sliced peeled potatoes
1 cup sliced onion
3 tablespoons bacon drippings

Combine potatoes and onion; season with salt and pepper. In skillet cook, covered, in drippings for 10 minutes. Uncover; turn and cook potatoes on the other side 5 to 10 minutes, loosening occasionally. Makes 6 to 8 servings.

Scalloped Potatoes

6 to 8 medium potatoes, peeled
and thinly sliced (6 cups)
¼ cup finely chopped onion
⅓ cup all-purpose flour
1½ teaspoons salt
⅛ teaspoon pepper
2 cups milk

Place *half* the potatoes in a greased 2-quart casserole. Add *half* the onion. Sift *half* the flour over; sprinkle with *half* the salt and pepper. Repeat layers. Pour milk over all. If desired, sprinkle top with 3 tablespoons buttered fine dry bread crumbs. Cover and bake at 350° for 1¼ hours. Uncover; continue baking till potatoes are done, 15 to 30 minutes longer. Makes 6 servings.

Grilled Potato and Onion Bake

4 large baking potatoes, peeled
2 medium onions
⅓ cup grated Parmesan cheese
Salt
Pepper
2 tablespoons butter *or*
margarine

Slice potatoes and onions onto a 24x18-inch sheet of buttered heavy-duty foil. Sprinkle with Parmesan cheese, salt, and pepper; mix lightly on foil. Slice the 2 tablespoons butter over all. Seal foil with double fold. Place on grill; cook over *slow* coals till vegetables are tender, 50 to 55 minutes, turning often. Makes 6 servings.

Vichyssoise

4 leeks, sliced (without tops)
1 medium onion, sliced
¼ cup butter *or* margarine
5 medium potatoes, peeled
and thinly sliced
4 cups chicken broth
1 tablespoon salt
2 cups milk
2 cups light cream
1 cup whipping cream
Snipped chives

In saucepan cook leeks and onion in butter or margarine till tender but not brown. Add potatoes, broth, and salt. Cook for 35 to 40 minutes. Rub through very fine sieve, or place in blender container; cover and blend till smooth.

Return to heat; add milk and light cream. Season to taste with salt and pepper. Bring to boiling. Cool. Stir in whipping cream. Chill thoroughly before serving. Garnish with snipped chives. Makes 8 servings.

Crunch-Top Potatoes

¼ cup butter *or* margarine,
melted
2 16-ounce cans sliced potatoes,
drained
1 cup shredded Cheddar
cheese (4 ounces)
¾ cup crushed cornflakes
1 teaspoon paprika

Pour butter into 13x9x2-inch baking pan. Add potatoes in single layer; turn once in butter. Combine cheese, crushed cornflakes, and paprika; sprinkle over potatoes. Bake at 375° about 20 minutes. Makes 6 servings.

Potatoes and Eggs au Gratin

4 medium potatoes (1½ pounds)
¼ cup chopped onion
1 tablespoon butter *or* margarine
3 tablespoons all-purpose flour
1 cup dairy sour cream
¾ cup shredded sharp American
    cheese (3 ounces)
½ cup milk
2 tablespoons snipped parsley
1 teaspoon salt
⅛ teaspoon paprika
⅛ teaspoon pepper
4 hard-cooked eggs, sliced
1 large tomato, peeled and cut
    in small wedges
¾ cup soft bread crumbs (1 slice)
1 tablespoon butter *or* margarine,
    melted

In covered pan cook whole potatoes in enough boiling salted water to cover till almost tender, 20 to 25 minutes; drain. Peel and slice cooked potatoes (should have about 3 cups).

Meanwhile, in saucepan cook onion in 1 tablespoon butter or margarine till tender. Blend in flour. Stir in sour cream, shredded cheese, milk, parsley, salt, paprika, and pepper. Cook and stir over low heat till cheese melts. Combine sour cream mixture and sliced potatoes.

In 1½-quart casserole spread *half* the potato mixture. Top with egg slices and tomato wedges. Spoon remaining potato mixture atop. Toss bread crumbs with the melted butter; sprinkle atop. Bake at 350° for 45 to 50 minutes. Garnish with additional tomato wedges, hard-cooked egg wedges, and parsley, if desired. Makes 4 servings.

German-Style New Potato Salad

1 pound tiny new potatoes
2 cups torn lettuce
1 cup torn curly endive
2 hard-cooked eggs, chopped
¼ cup thinly sliced radishes
3 tablespoons sliced green onion
    with tops
6 slices bacon
⅓ cup vinegar
1 teaspoon seasoned salt
¼ teaspoon celery seed
⅛ teaspoon pepper

Peel strip around center of each potato. Cook potatoes in boiling water as directed on page 70. Drain. Halve any large potatoes. In bowl combine cooked potatoes, lettuce, curly endive, eggs, radishes, and green onion.

In skillet cook bacon till crisp. Drain, reserving ⅓ cup drippings. Crumble bacon; add to potato mixture. To reserved drippings in skillet add vinegar, seasoned salt, celery seed, and pepper. Heat to boiling; pour over potato mixture. Toss quickly; serve at once. Makes 4 to 6 servings.

Calico Potato Salad

7 medium potatoes, cooked,
    peeled, and cubed
½ cup chopped cucumber
½ cup chopped onion
¼ cup chopped green pepper
3 tablespoons chopped pimiento
1½ teaspoons salt
¾ teaspoon celery seed
¼ teaspoon pepper
2 hard-cooked eggs
⅓ cup mayonnaise *or* salad
    dressing
3 tablespoons vinegar
2 tablespoons sugar
1 tablespoon prepared mustard
½ cup whipping cream
    Lettuce

Stir together cubed potatoes, cucumber, onion, green pepper, pimiento, salt, celery seed, and pepper. Reserve 1 hard-cooked egg yolk. Coarsely chop the white and remaining hard-cooked egg. Add chopped eggs to potato mixture; chill. Blend mayonnaise or salad dressing, vinegar, sugar, and mustard; whip cream and fold into mayonnaise mixture. About ½ hour before serving, toss with potato mixture. To serve, spoon into lettuce-lined bowl. Sieve the reserved egg yolk over salad. Makes 6 servings.

Vary the potato course of the menu with hearty, layered *Potatoes and Eggs au Gratin,* or
German-Style New Potato Salad enhanced by bacon and lettuce and spiked with a zesty dressing.

French Fries

Baking potatoes, peeled
Fat for deep-fat frying
Salt

Cut potatoes lengthwise in ⅜-inch-wide strips. Fry potatoes, a few at a time, in deep hot fat (360°) till crisp and golden, 6 to 7 minutes. Drain on paper toweling. (For crisper French fries, fry potatoes at 360° till lightly browned, about 5 minutes. Drain on paper toweling and cool. Just before serving, return French fries to fat at 360° for 2 minutes more.) Sprinkle potatoes immediately with salt. Serve at once.

Potato Salad Roll

3 medium potatoes, peeled and
    quartered
⅓ cup mayonnaise
1 teaspoon salt
½ teaspoon paprika
3 hard-cooked eggs, finely
    chopped
½ cup chopped celery
2 tablespoons finely chopped
    onion
1 cup cream-style cottage cheese
2 tablespoons finely chopped
    green pepper
2 tablespoons chopped pimiento
2 tablespoons mayonnaise

Cook potatoes in boiling water as directed on page 70. Mash potatoes; *do not add liquid*. Combine mashed potatoes, the ⅓ cup mayonnaise, salt, and paprika; stir in eggs, celery, and onion. Chill thoroughly.

Pat potato mixture on foil to a 12x9-inch rectangle. Drain cottage cheese. Combine cottage cheese, green pepper, pimiento, and the 2 tablespoons mayonnaise; spread atop potato mixture to within 1 inch of edges. Beginning with narrow side, lift foil and gently roll up potato mixture jelly-roll fashion. Chill thoroughly. Cut well-chilled potato roll into slices. Makes 6 servings.

Twice-Baked Potatoes

4 medium baking potatoes
2 tablespoons butter *or*
    margarine
  Milk
1 2-ounce can chopped
    mushrooms, drained
2 slices American cheese,
    halved diagonally
  Paprika

Scrub potatoes thoroughly and prick with a fork. Bake potatoes as directed on page 70.

Cut a lengthwise slice from top of each potato; discard skin from slice. Reserving potato shells, scoop out the insides and add to potato portions from top slices; mash. Add butter. Beat in enough milk to make a stiff consistency. Season to taste with salt and pepper. Stir in mushrooms.

Pile mashed potato mixture into potato shells. Place in 10x6x2-inch baking dish. Return to oven; bake at 425° till lightly browned, 20 to 25 minutes. Place cheese atop potatoes; sprinkle with paprika. Bake till cheese melts, 2 to 3 minutes longer. Makes 4 servings.

Microwave cooking directions: Scrub potatoes; prick with fork. In countertop microwave oven arrange potatoes on paper toweling, leaving at least 1 inch between potatoes. Micro-cook, uncovered, till potatoes are done, 13 to 15 minutes for four potatoes. (Allow 6 to 8 minutes for two potatoes; 17 to 19 minutes for six potatoes.) Halfway through cooking time, rearrange potatoes and turn over.

Prepare potato shells and mashed potato mixture as above. Pile mashed potato mixture into potato shells. Place in 10x6x2-inch nonmetal baking dish. Micro-cook, uncovered, till potatoes are heated through, about 5 minutes, rearranging potatoes twice. Place cheese atop potatoes. Sprinkle with paprika. Micro-cook 30 seconds longer.

Spinach

Selecting: Look for large, fresh-looking leaves, and avoid spinach that's wilted or yellowed. Store covered in the refrigerator crisper and plan to use soon after purchasing.

Preparing: It's important to wash spinach thoroughly to remove sand particles. Rather than washing each leaf separately under cold water, place the leaves in a pan of lukewarm water. After a few minutes, lift out and drain leaves; discard the water. Repeat until no sand collects in the pan. To crisp the leaves, add crushed ice to spinach and refrigerate about 1 hour.

Cooking: For best flavor, cook spinach with a very small amount of water. In fact, if you use a tightly covered saucepan, you can cook spinach with only the water that clings to the leaves. Reduce heat when steam begins to form, and cook 3 to 5 minutes longer. Turn leaves frequently while cooking.

Serving: Torn raw spinach is attractive and delicious in tossed salads. Add allspice, basil, cinnamon, or nutmeg to spinach while cooking.

Chinese Spinach

1 pound spinach (12 cups)
2 tablespoons cooking oil
2 tablespoons soy sauce
½ teaspoon sugar
½ cup sliced water chestnuts
2 tablespoons chopped onion

Cut fresh spinach stems into 1-inch pieces; tear leaves into bite-size pieces. In large covered saucepan simmer spinach with a small amount of water for 3 minutes; drain well. Heat oil, soy, and sugar in skillet; add spinach, water chestnuts, and onion. Cook and toss till spinach is well-coated and heated through, 2 to 3 minutes. Makes 4 servings.

Scalloped Spinach

2 10-ounce packages frozen
  chopped spinach
¾ cup milk
¾ cup shredded American cheese
3 beaten eggs
3 tablespoons chopped onion
1 cup soft bread crumbs
1 tablespoon butter, melted

Cook spinach according to package directions; drain well. Mix with milk, ½ cup of the cheese, eggs, onion, ½ teaspoon salt, and dash pepper. Turn into greased 8x8x2-inch baking pan. Bake at 350° for 25 minutes. Combine crumbs, remaining cheese, and butter; sprinkle atop spinach. Bake till knife inserted off-center comes out clean, 10 to 15 minutes longer. Let stand 5 minutes before serving. Makes 6 servings.

Japanese Custard Soup

6 small raw shrimp, peeled and
   deveined
6 spinach leaves, cut into 1½-
   inch pieces
⅓ cup sliced fresh mushrooms
   (1 ounce)
6 water chestnuts, sliced
2 slightly beaten eggs
1 13¾-ounce can chicken broth
¼ teaspoon salt

Make small slit in each shrimp; pull tail through. Pour hot water over spinach to wilt; drain. Divide and arrange shrimp, spinach, mushrooms, and water chestnuts in six 6-ounce custard cups or Chawan-Mushi cups.

Combine eggs, broth, and salt; pour into cups. Cover each cup with foil; set on wire rack in Dutch oven or deep skillet. Pour hot water around cups to depth of 1 inch on cup sides; cover Dutch oven or skillet. Over medium heat bring water to simmering. Reduce heat; cook till knife inserted off-center comes out clean, about 10 minutes. Makes 6 servings.

Wilted Spinach Salad

½ pound spinach (6 cups)
¼ cup sliced green onion with
   tops
   Dash freshly ground pepper
2 or 3 slices bacon
1 tablespoon white wine vinegar
2 teaspoons lemon juice
½ teaspoon sugar
1 hard-cooked egg, chopped

Wash fresh spinach and pat dry on paper toweling; tear into a bowl. Add green onion; sprinkle with pepper. Chill. Cut bacon into small pieces. In large chafing dish or skillet cook bacon till crisp. Blend in vinegar, lemon juice, sugar, and ¼ teaspoon salt. Gradually add spinach and green onion, tossing just till spinach is coated and wilted slightly, 3 to 5 minutes. Turn into serving dish; sprinkle with chopped hard-cooked egg. Makes 4 servings.

Herbed Spinach Bake

1 10-ounce package frozen
   chopped spinach
2 tablespoons butter
1 cup cooked rice
1 cup shredded American cheese
⅓ cup milk
2 slightly beaten eggs
2 tablespoons chopped onion
½ teaspoon Worcestershire sauce
¼ teaspoon dried rosemary,
   crushed

Cook the spinach according to package directions; drain well. Stir in butter till melted. Stir in rice, shredded cheese, milk, eggs, onion, Worcestershire sauce, rosemary, and ½ teaspoon salt. Pour mixture into 10x6x2-inch baking dish. Bake at 350° till knife inserted halfway between center and edge comes out clean, 30 to 35 minutes. Cut into squares to serve. Makes 6 servings.

Cottage Cheese-Spinach Salad

½ cup dairy sour cream
2 tablespoons sugar
1 tablespoon prepared
   horseradish
½ teaspoon dry mustard
¼ teaspoon salt
3 tablespoons herb-flavored
   vinegar
10 ounces spinach (7 cups)
1½ cups cream-style cottage
   cheese
½ cup chopped walnuts

Stir together sour cream, sugar, horseradish, dry mustard, and salt. Gradually blend in vinegar. Cover and chill.

Tear fresh spinach into bite-size pieces. Arrange spinach in salad bowl; top with cottage cheese and chopped walnuts. Pour sour cream mixture over; toss lightly to coat spinach. Makes 6 to 8 servings.

Squash (winter)

Selecting: Winter squash is the common name for mature, hard-shelled varieties such as acorn, banana, butternut, turban, Hubbard, and buttercup squash. Choose squash that are heavy for their size, with hard rinds and good coloring and shaping for the variety. Large banana or Hubbard squash are sometimes cut into pieces and sold by the pound. Avoid pieces that are discolored or don't appear fresh.

Preparing: Although you can peel squash before cooking, it's much easier to cook it and then remove the peel. Unless very small, halve the squash and remove the seeds and strings before cooking. Cut the squash into serving-size pieces, rings, or cubes.

Cooking: For baked squash, place halves or serving-size pieces, cut side down, in baking pan. Cover with foil; bake at 350° for 30 minutes. Turn cut side up; bake, covered, till tender (20 to 30 minutes more for acorn, buttercup, or butternut squash; 45 to 50 minutes more for Hubbard, banana, or spaghetti squash). Or, in covered pan cook squash in small amount of boiling salted water (allow 15 minutes for cubes).

Serving: For a hearty main dish, serve meat-stuffed squash pieces. Try spaghetti squash with butter or spaghetti sauce. To serve the other winter squash as a vegetable, simply fill the cavities with butter and brown sugar or honey.

Sausage-Stuffed Turban Squash (pictured on pages 4-5)

1 3-pound turban squash
Salt
1 pound bulk pork sausage
1 cup chopped celery
½ cup sliced fresh mushrooms
¼ cup chopped onion
1 slightly beaten egg
½ cup dairy sour cream
¼ cup grated Parmesan cheese
¼ teaspoon salt

Cut slice from stem end of squash so squash will stand upright. Cut out turban end; scoop out seeds. Lightly salt inside of squash. Place squash, scooped end down, in shallow baking pan. Bake at 375° till tender, about 1 hour.

Meanwhile, in skillet combine pork sausage, celery, mushrooms, and onion; cook till vegetables are tender and meat is brown. Drain well. Combine egg, sour cream, Parmesan cheese, and the ¼ teaspoon salt. Stir into sausage mixture. Turn squash scooped end up; fill with sausage mixture. Bake 20 to 25 minutes longer. Makes 6 servings.

Simple but delicious describes *Candied Squash Rings.* Acorn squash and an easy brown sugar-and-butter glaze are all you need for the conventional or microwave version of this recipe.

Candied Squash Rings

2 **acorn squash**
 Salt
 Pepper
½ **cup packed brown sugar**
¼ **cup butter** *or* **margarine**
2 **tablespoons water**

Cut squash crosswise into 1-inch slices; discard seeds. Arrange in single layer in shallow baking pan; season with salt and pepper. Cover and bake at 350° till almost tender, about 40 minutes. In saucepan combine brown sugar, butter, and water; cook and stir till bubbly. Spoon over squash. Continue baking, uncovered, till squash is tender, about 15 minutes more, basting often. Makes 4 to 6 servings.

Microwave cooking directions: Pierce squash with metal skewer in several places. Cook in countertop microwave oven till soft, 8 to 10 minutes. Let stand 5 minutes. Cut crosswise into 1-inch slices; discard seeds. Place squash in 12x 7½x2-inch nonmetal baking dish. Season with salt and pepper. In glass measuring cup combine remaining ingredients. Micro-cook 15 *seconds*. Spoon over squash. Cover with waxed paper. Micro-cook till hot, 3 to 5 minutes; baste once.

Squash Soufflé (pictured on pages 4-5)

3 cups mashed cooked winter
   squash
¼ cup butter *or* margarine
2 tablespoons brown sugar
½ teaspoon salt
½ teaspoon finely shredded
   orange peel
⅛ teaspoon ground nutmeg
   Dash pepper
4 egg yolks
4 stiffly beaten egg whites

In large mixing bowl combine squash, butter or margarine, brown sugar, salt, orange peel, nutmeg, and pepper. Beat till fluffy. Add egg yolks; beat well. Carefully fold squash mixture into stiffly beaten egg whites. Turn into 1½-quart soufflé dish. Bake soufflé at 350° till set, 55 to 60 minutes. Makes 8 to 10 servings.

Bean and Squash Soup

1 pound dry navy beans (2⅓ cups)
8 cups water
2 pounds winter squash, peeled,
   seeded, and cubed
   (about 4 cups)
1 meaty ham bone (about 1 pound)
1 cup chopped onion
1 cup chopped celery
1½ teaspoons salt
¼ teaspoon pepper

In 5-quart Dutch oven combine navy beans and water. Cover and soak overnight. (Or, bring to boiling; reduce heat and simmer 2 minutes. Remove from heat. Cover and let stand 1 hour.) *Do not drain.* Add *half* the winter squash, the ham bone, onion, celery, salt, and pepper. Bring to boiling. Reduce heat; cover and simmer 1½ hours. Remove ham bone; cool slightly. Partially mash beans with potato masher. Cut meat from ham bone. Chop meat; return to Dutch oven along with remaining winter squash. Simmer, covered, 20 minutes longer. Season to taste. Makes 8 to 10 servings.

Saucy Dilled Winter Squash

2 pounds winter squash,
   seeded and cubed (4 cups)
2 tablespoons sliced green onion
   with tops
1 tablespoon butter *or* margarine
½ cup dairy sour cream
2 tablespoons milk
¼ teaspoon salt
   Dash pepper
¼ teaspoon dried dillweed

Cook squash in boiling water as directed on page 77; drain well. Peel squash. Cook onion in butter till tender; blend in sour cream, milk, salt, and pepper. Heat through, but *do not boil.* Arrange squash on serving plate; top with sour cream mixture. Sprinkle with dillweed. Makes 6 servings.

Shaker Squash

1 2½- to 3-pound Hubbard squash,
   cut in large pieces
2 tablespoons maple *or*
   maple-flavored syrup
2 tablespoons butter
1 teaspoon salt
   Dash pepper
1 tablespoon snipped parsley *or*
   sliced green onion with tops

Place squash pieces in large baking pan. Bake, covered, at 350° till tender, about 1¼ hours. Remove pulp; press through sieve. Place pulp in saucepan; stir in syrup, butter, salt, and pepper. Heat through. (If thin, cook and stir till desired consistency.) Top with snipped parsley or sliced onion. Makes 6 to 8 servings.

Sweet Potatoes & Yams

Selecting: Sweet potatoes range in skin color from light yellow to orange to copper, and in flesh color from light yellow to red-orange. In this country, "yam" is used interchangeably with "sweet potato" and refers particularly to a sweet potato variety with copper skin and orange flesh. Uniform shape, uniform skin color, and firmness are characteristics to look for when selecting sweet potatoes. Don't choose decayed, soft, or shriveled vegetables. Store sweet potatoes in a cool (about 55°), dry place rather than in the refrigerator, and plan to use them within a few days.

Preparing: Scrub sweet potatoes; remove ends and woody portions. Peel sweet potatoes before or after cooking, depending on their use.

Cooking: Bake whole sweet potatoes at 375° for 40 to 45 minutes; allow a little less time for thickly sliced sweet potatoes. Or, in covered pan cook whole sweet potatoes in enough boiling salted water to cover till tender, 30 to 40 minutes.

Serving: Baked, mashed, or candied—sweet potatoes are a holiday tradition. Marshmallows are the perfect topping for a sweet potato casserole. Sweet potato pie, bread, and biscuits are also favorites, particularly in the South.

Sweet Potato-Cashew Bake

½ cup packed brown sugar
⅓ cup broken cashews
½ teaspoon salt
¼ teaspoon ground ginger
2 pounds sweet potatoes (5 or 6 medium), cooked, peeled, and cut crosswise into thick pieces
1 8-ounce can peach slices, well drained
3 tablespoons butter or margarine

Combine brown sugar, cashews, salt, and ginger. In 10x6x2-inch baking dish layer *half* the sweet potatoes, *half* the peach slices, and *half* the brown sugar mixture. Repeat layers. Dot with butter or margarine. Bake, covered, at 350° for 30 minutes. Uncover and bake mixture about 10 minutes longer. Spoon brown sugar syrup over before serving. Makes 6 to 8 servings.

Glazed sweet potatoes are enhanced by cashews and canned peach slices in golden
Sweet Potato-Cashew Bake. Include this recipe in your Thanksgiving menu. It's sure to be a hit.

Raisin-Filled Sweet Potatoes

1 17-ounce can sweet potatoes, drained
2 tablespoons butter, softened
1 egg
½ teaspoon salt
Dash ground cinnamon
Dash ground ginger
2 tablespoons butter, melted
¼ cup sugar
2 teaspoons cornstarch
1 teaspoon finely shredded orange peel
½ cup orange juice
½ cup raisins

Beat together drained sweet potatoes, the softened butter, egg, salt, cinnamon, and ginger. Spoon into 6 mounds on a greased baking sheet. Make depressions in centers with spoon. Brush with the melted butter. Bake at 350° for 15 to 20 minutes. In saucepan combine sugar, cornstarch, and peel. Stir in orange juice and raisins. Cook and stir till thickened and bubbly. To serve, spoon raisin mixture into depressions in potato mounds. Makes 6 servings.

Candied Sweet Potato Boats

4 small sweet potatoes
½ cup prepared mincemeat
3 tablespoons butter *or* margarine
1 tablespoon lemon juice
½ teaspoon salt
¼ cup chopped pecans

Scrub sweet potatoes with brush. Bake as directed on page 80. Remove from oven; reduce oven temperature to 325°. Cut potatoes in half lengthwise. Scoop out center of halves, leaving about ½-inch shell; set shells aside. In a mixing bowl mash centers; stir in mincemeat, butter, lemon juice, and salt. Sprinkle shells lightly with additional salt; spoon mashed potato mixture into potato shells. Sprinkle pecans over potatoes. Return to oven and bake at 325° till heated through, about 15 minutes longer. Makes 8 servings.

Apricot-Sauced Sweets

1 cup snipped dried apricots
¾ cup orange juice
½ cup water
3 tablespoons brown sugar
2 tablespoons honey
2 tablespoons butter
2½ pounds sweet potatoes, cooked, peeled, and cut crosswise into thick pieces
½ cup walnut halves

In saucepan combine apricots, orange juice, water, brown sugar, and honey. Bring to boiling. Reduce heat; cover and simmer till apricots are tender, 20 to 25 minutes. Remove from heat and stir in butter.

Arrange sweet potatoes in a 12-inch skillet; sprinkle with walnuts. Pour apricot sauce over. Cover and simmer till potatoes are heated through and glazed, about 15 minutes. Baste frequently. Makes 12 servings.

Sweet Potato Biscuits

1¼ cups all-purpose flour
1 tablespoon baking powder
2 teaspoons brown sugar
½ teaspoon salt
⅓ cup shortening
1 beaten egg
½ cup mashed cooked sweet potato
2 tablespoons milk

In mixing bowl stir together the flour, baking powder, brown sugar, and salt. Cut in shortening till mixture resembles coarse crumbs. Combine egg, mashed sweet potato, and milk; add all at once to dry mixture. Stir just till dough clings together. Knead gently on lightly floured surface (10 to 12 strokes). Roll or pat dough to ½-inch thickness. Cut with 2½-inch biscuit cutter, dipping cutter in flour between cuts. Place on ungreased baking sheet. Bake at 425° for 10 to 12 minutes. Makes 8 biscuits.

Tomatoes

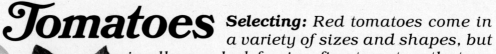

Selecting: *Red tomatoes come in a variety of sizes and shapes, but in all cases look for ripe, firm tomatoes that are unblemished and well-shaped. Tomatoes that aren't quite ripe will ripen if left at 60° to 70° out of direct light. Store fully ripe tomatoes in the refrigerator crisper and use within a few days.*

Preparing: *Wash and remove stems. If a tomato has a large core, cut it out. Tomatoes peel easily by spearing with a fork and immersing in boiling water for about 30 seconds. Remove from boiling water and immediately place tomato in cold water. When cool, slip off the skin. Or, spear the tomato with a fork and rotate it over an open flame till the skin wrinkles slightly; then cool and peel.*

Cooking: *For stewed tomatoes, place peeled whole or cut-up tomatoes in saucepan. Tightly cover and cook over low heat till done, 10 to 15 minutes (do not add water). Season stewed tomatoes with salt, pepper, and a little sugar.*

Serving: *Whole raw tomato cups stuffed with a meat or seafood salad make a refreshing luncheon entrée. Tomato wedges are a favorite salad ingredient. Tomatoes are also delicious broiled, stewed, or scalloped. Green (unripe) tomatoes are sometimes fried, pickled, or used for pies.*

Huevos Rancheros

¼ cup cooking oil
6 frozen tortillas, thawed
½ cup chopped onion
1 small clove garlic, minced
2 tablespoons cooking oil
3 large tomatoes, peeled
   and finely chopped
2 canned green chili peppers,
   drained, seeded, and
   chopped (¼ cup)
¼ teaspoon salt
6 eggs
1 cup shredded Monterey Jack
   cheese (4 ounces)

Heat the ¼ cup oil in a small skillet. Dip tortillas in oil for a few seconds till softened but not brown. Keep warm. In medium skillet cook onion and garlic in the 2 tablespoons oil till onion is tender but not brown. Add tomatoes, chili peppers, and salt. Simmer 10 minutes.

Carefully break eggs, one at a time, into a small bowl. Slide each egg into tomato mixture, taking care not to break yolk. Season with salt and pepper. Cover skillet and cook eggs till desired doneness. Place an egg with some of the tomato mixture on each tortilla. Sprinkle shredded Monterey Jack cheese atop eggs. Makes 6 servings.

Scalloped Tomatoes

2 pounds tomatoes, peeled
    and cut up (6 medium), *or*
    1 28-ounce can tomatoes,
    cut up
1 cup sliced celery
½ cup chopped onion
2 tablespoons all-purpose flour
1 tablespoon sugar
½ teaspoon salt
½ teaspoon dried marjoram,
    crushed
    Dash pepper
¼ cup water
2 tablespoons butter
4 slices bread, toasted
2 tablespoons grated Parmesan
    cheese

In saucepan combine fresh or canned tomatoes, celery, and onion. Cover and bring to boiling; reduce heat. Simmer, covered, till celery is tender, about 10 minutes. Combine flour, sugar, salt, marjoram, and pepper. Blend in water; stir into tomatoes. Cook, stirring constantly, till thickened and bubbly. Stir in butter till melted.

Cut 3 *slices* toast into cubes; stir into tomato mixture. Pour into a 1½-quart casserole or a 10x6x2-inch baking dish. Bake at 350° for 30 minutes. Cut the remaining slice of toast into 4 triangles. Arrange triangles down center of tomato mixture, overlapping slightly. Sprinkle with Parmesan cheese. Bake 20 minutes longer. Serve scalloped tomatoes in sauce dishes. Makes 6 servings.

Herbed Fresh Tomato Soup

2 tablespoons butter
2 tablespoons olive oil *or*
    cooking oil
2 medium onions, thinly sliced
2 pound tomatoes, peeled and
    quartered (6 medium)
1 6-ounce can tomato paste
2 tablespoons snipped fresh
    basil *or* 2 teaspoons dried
    basil, crushed
4 teaspoons snipped fresh thyme
    or 1 teaspoon dried thyme,
    crushed
1 tablespoon instant chicken
    bouillon granules
3 cups water
1 teaspoon salt
⅛ teaspoon pepper

In large saucepan heat butter and oil till butter melts. Add onions; cook till tender but not brown. Stir in tomatoes, tomato paste, basil, thyme, and bouillon granules; mash tomatoes slightly. Stir in water; bring to boiling. Reduce heat; cover and simmer for 40 minutes. Press through food mill. (*Or*, place a small amount at a time in blender; cover and blend till pureed. Repeat with remaining mixture.) Strain mixture. Return to saucepan; stir in salt and pepper. Heat through. Pour into soup tureen or ladle into individual soup bowls. Garnish with celery tops, if desired. Makes 8 servings.

Salsa

4 medium tomatoes, peeled
    and chopped
½ cup chopped onion
½ cup chopped celery
¼ cup chopped green pepper
¼ cup olive oil *or* cooking oil
2 to 3 tablespoons chopped
    canned green chili peppers
2 tablespoons red wine vinegar
1 teaspoon mustard seed
1 teaspoon coriander seed,
    crushed

Combine tomatoes, onion, celery, green pepper, olive or cooking oil, green chili peppers, vinegar, mustard seed, coriander seed, 1 teaspoon salt, and dash pepper. Cover; refrigerate several hours or overnight, stirring occasionally. Garnish with green pepper strips, if desired. Serve as a relish. Makes about 3 cups.

The popular tomato crops up in a wide variety of tasty dishes. Old-fashioned *Scalloped Tomatoes*, *Herbed Fresh Tomato Soup*, and Mexican-style *Salsa* are three long-standing favorites.

Tomato Spaghetti Sauce

1 cup finely chopped onion
2 cloves garlic, minced
2 tablespoons cooking oil
    (conventional method only)
2 pounds tomatoes, peeled and
    cut up, *or* 1 28-ounce can
    tomatoes, cut up
1 6-ounce can tomato paste
1 tablespoon sugar
2 teaspoons instant beef
    bouillon granules
1 teaspoon dried oregano, crushed
½ teaspoon dried basil, crushed
1 large bay leaf
1 4-ounce can sliced mushrooms
2 tablespoons cornstarch
    (crockery cooker method only)
    Hot cooked spaghetti

In 3-quart saucepan cook onion and garlic in oil. Add tomatoes, tomato paste, sugar, bouillon granules, oregano, basil, bay leaf, ½ teaspoon salt, and ⅛ teaspoon pepper. Stir in 1½ cups water. Bring to boiling. Reduce heat and simmer, uncovered, for 1¼ to 1½ hours, stirring occasionally. Remove bay leaf. Stir in mushrooms; simmer till desired consistency, 15 to 30 minutes more. Serve over spaghetti; pass grated Parmesan cheese, if desired. Makes 6 servings.

Crockery cooker directions: In electric slow crockery cooker combine onion, garlic, tomatoes, tomato paste, sugar, bouillon granules, oregano, basil, bay leaf, ½ teaspoon salt, and ⅛ teaspoon pepper (omit cooking oil). Stir in 1½ cups water. Cover; cook on low-heat setting for 10 to 12 hours. Turn to high-heat setting. Remove bay leaf; stir in mushrooms. Blend 2 tablespoons cold water into the 2 tablespoons cornstarch; stir into sauce. Cover; cook till thickened and bubbly, about 25 minutes. Serve as above.

Vera Cruz Tomatoes

3 slices bacon
¼ cup chopped onion
½ pound spinach, snipped
½ cup dairy sour cream
    Dash bottled hot pepper sauce
4 medium tomatoes
½ cup shredded mozzarella
    cheese (2 ounces)

Cook bacon till crisp. Drain; reserve 2 tablespoons drippings. Crumble bacon; set aside. Cook onion in drippings; stir in fresh spinach. Cover; cook till tender, 3 to 5 minutes. Remove from heat; stir in sour cream, pepper sauce, and bacon. Cut tops off tomatoes. Remove centers, leaving shells; drain. Sprinkle shells with salt; fill with spinach mixture. Bake in 8x8x2-inch baking pan at 375° for 20 to 25 minutes. Top with cheese; heat till cheese melts. Makes 4 servings.

Marinated Herbed Tomatoes

6 tomatoes
⅔ cup salad oil
¼ cup vinegar
¼ cup *each* snipped parsley and
    sliced green onion with tops
½ teaspoon dried marjoram,
    crushed

Peel tomatoes; place in a deep bowl. In a screw-top jar combine oil, vinegar, parsley, green onion, marjoram, 1 teaspoon salt, and ¼ teaspoon pepper. Shake well. Pour over tomatoes. Cover and refrigerate several hours or overnight, spooning herb mixture over tomatoes occasionally. At serving time, spoon herb mixture over tomatoes again. If desired, serve on lettuce-lined platter. Makes 6 servings.

Tomato Aspic

4 medium tomatoes
2 ribs celery, sliced
¼ small onion
2 tablespoons brown sugar
2 tablespoons lemon juice
½ teaspoon salt
½ teaspoon celery salt
    Dash bottled hot pepper sauce
2 envelopes unflavored gelatin

Peel and quarter tomatoes; place in blender container. Cover; blend till pureed. Add celery, onion, brown sugar, lemon juice, salt, celery salt, and hot pepper sauce. Cover; blend till vegetables are finely chopped.

In small saucepan soften gelatin in ¾ cup cold water. Place over low heat and stir till gelatin is dissolved. Stir in tomato mixture; chill till partially set. Turn into 4½-cup ring mold. Chill till firm. Makes 8 servings.

Canned Tomatoes

15 pounds firm, ripe tomatoes (select tomatoes of about the same size)
Salt (¼ teaspoon for each pint; ½ teaspoon for each quart)

Peel tomatoes. Cut out stem ends and cores. Pack small or medium tomatoes whole; cut large tomatoes in quarters or eighths. Scrape out seeds with spoon, if desired. For *raw pack*, pack tomatoes into hot, clean jars, pressing gently; leave ½-inch headspace. Add salt. For *hot pack*, bring tomatoes to a boil; stir constantly but gently. Pack hot tomatoes into hot, clean jars; leave ½-inch headspace. Add salt.

Prepare lids according to manufacturer's directions. Wipe jar rim. Adjust lid on jar. *Process raw pack* tomatoes in boiling water bath 35 minutes for pints; 45 minutes for quarts. *Process hot pack* tomatoes in boiling water bath for 10 minutes for pints and quarts (start timing raw or hot pack when water returns to boil). Makes 6 quarts.

Canned Tomato Juice

9 pounds firm, ripe tomatoes
1 tablespoon lemon juice
Salt (¼ teaspoon for each pint; ½ teaspoon for each quart)

Cut up tomatoes, discarding stem ends and cores. Measure about 20 cups. In covered 8- to 10-quart kettle slowly cook tomatoes till soft, about 15 minutes; stir often. Press through food mill or sieve to extract juice; measure 12 cups juice. Return juice to kettle; bring to boil. Stir in lemon juice. Pour hot juice into hot, clean jars; leave ½-inch headspace. Add salt. Prepare lids according to manufacturer's directions. Wipe jar rim. Adjust lid. Process jars in boiling water bath for 10 minutes for pints; 15 minutes for quarts (start timing when water returns to boil). Makes 6 pints.

Green Tomato Pickles

4 pounds green tomatoes
4 medium onions, sliced
1 cup chopped green pepper
8 cups white vinegar
5 cups sugar
¼ cup mustard seed
1 tablespoon celery seed
1 teaspoon ground turmeric

Core tomatoes and slice ¼ inch thick. Measure 16 cups. Combine tomatoes, onions, and green pepper; set aside. In saucepan combine remaining ingredients; bring to boil. Pack vegetables into hot, clean pint jars; leave ½-inch headspace. Pour hot liquid over vegetables; leave ½-inch headspace.

Prepare lids according to manufacturer's directions. Wipe jar rim. Adjust lid. Process jars in boiling water bath 15 minutes (start timing when water returns to boil). Makes 8 pints.

Water-bath Canning Tips

Process tomatoes and vegetables made into sauerkraut, relishes, and pickles (see tip, page 40) in a water-bath canner. The 212° temperature reached at sea level in the boiling water bath sufficiently destroys organisms that cause spoilage in tomatoes. Sauerkraut, relishes, and pickles are prepared with vinegar and/or brine to preserve the product. In high-altitude areas, check with the county extension agent for altitude corrections. *Do not can* overripe tomatoes or those with soft spots or decay. The acid content of overripe tomatoes is lower than that of firm, ripe tomatoes. This may interfere with the tomatoes' keeping quality.

Turnips & Rutabagas

Selecting: Turnips and rutabagas are most plentiful in the fall and winter. The best-known turnip variety is raised for its bulbous root, identified by a purple-collared white skin. Some varieties do not form an enlarged root, but are grown mainly for the leaves (see Greens). Rutabagas are larger than turnips and slightly elongated. The yellow-fleshed varieties are most common. Select smooth, firm turnips and rutabagas of small or medium size. An edible wax coating is sometimes applied to preserve freshness. Turnips and rutabagas keep best stored in the refrigerator.

Preparing: Wash turnips and rutabagas and peel off outer skin. Slice or cube.

Cooking: In covered pan cook vegetable in small amount of boiling salted water till just tender. Allow 10 to 20 minutes for turnips; 20 to 35 minutes for rutabagas.

Serving: Include turnips or rutabagas in soups, pot roasts, and side dishes. Or, mash cooked vegetable like potatoes.

Lemon Turnips

3 medium turnips, peeled and
  cut into strips
2 tablespoons butter
1 tablespoon snipped parsley
1 teaspoon chopped onion
1 teaspoon lemon juice

Cook turnips as directed above; drain well. Add butter, snipped parsley, chopped onion, and lemon juice. Toss to coat. Season with salt and pepper. Makes 4 servings.

Rutabaga and Apple

1 medium rutabaga (1 pound),
  peeled and cubed
1 medium apple, peeled, cored,
  and sliced
⅓ cup packed brown sugar
2 tablespoons butter *or*
  margarine

Cook rutabaga as directed above; drain well. Place *half* the rutabaga and *half* the apple in a 1-quart casserole. Sprinkle with *half* the brown sugar; dot with *half* the butter. Sprinkle with salt. Repeat layers of rutabaga, apple, brown sugar, butter, and salt. Bake, covered, at 350° for 30 minutes. Makes 4 to 6 servings.

Zucchini & other summer squash

Selecting: *Soft-shelled varieties of squash—commonly called summer squash—include dark green zucchini, yellow crookneck, disk-shaped pattypan, and spaghetti squash. Choose young squash that are firm, well-formed, glossy, and heavy for their size. Avoid hard or dull-rinded squash. You can store summer squash in refrigerator crisper one or two days.*

Preparing: *Usually the tender, thin rinds of summer squash are not removed. Wash squash and cut off ends. Slice, cube, or halve lengthwise.*

Cooking: *In covered pan cook squash in small amount of boiling salted water till crisp-tender, 5 to 10 minutes. Or, sauté in butter.*

Serving: *Mild-flavored summer squash combine well with tomatoes, corn, and other vegetables. Marinate uncooked slices in a tangy salad dressing, or use the raw pieces in salads or as vegetable dippers. Squash halves perform a dual role as vegetable and serving dish when filled with stuffing.*

Summer Squash Casserole

- 2 pounds crookneck *or* zucchini squash, sliced ⅜ inch thick (7 cups)
- ¼ cup chopped onion
- 1 10¾-ounce can condensed cream of chicken soup
- 1 cup dairy sour cream
- 1 cup shredded carrot
- ¼ cup butter *or* margarine
- 2 cups herb-seasoned stuffing mix (about ½ of an 8-ounce package)

Cook summer squash with onion in boiling salted water as directed above. Drain well. Combine soup and sour cream; stir in carrot. Fold in drained squash and onion. Melt butter or margarine; toss with stuffing mix.

Spread *half* the stuffing mixture in a 12x7½x2-inch baking dish. Spoon vegetable mixture atop. Sprinkle with remaining stuffing mixture. Bake at 350° till heated through, 25 to 30 minutes. Makes 6 servings.

Microwave cooking directions: Combine squash and onion in a 12x7½x2-inch nonmetal baking dish. Add ¼ cup water. Cover and cook in countertop microwave oven till squash is crisp-tender, about 15 minutes; stir every 3 minutes. Drain well. Combine soup and sour cream; stir in carrot. Fold in squash and onion. In nonmetal bowl micro-melt butter about 30 seconds. Stir in stuffing mix. Spread *half* the stuffing mixture in same nonmetal baking dish. Continue assembling as above. Micro-cook, uncovered, till heated through, about 7 minutes; give dish a half-turn after 4 minutes.

Enliven an ordinary luncheon or supper with a distinctive entrée, *Egg-Stuffed Zucchini.*
Crisp-tender squash shells hold the colorful, rich-tasting scrambled egg and tomato mixture.

Egg-Stuffed Zucchini

4 medium zucchini squash
  (about 1½ pounds)
½ cup water
1 large tomato, chopped
2 tablespoons butter *or*
  margarine
3 beaten eggs
¼ teaspoon salt
  Dash pepper
½ cup shredded sharp American
  cheese (2 ounces)

Halve zucchini lengthwise. Scoop out pulp, leaving ¼-inch shell. Chop pulp to make 1 cup; set aside. Place zucchini shells, cut side down, in large skillet. Add the water. Simmer, covered, till just tender, 5 to 6 minutes. Drain; turn cut side up in same skillet. Sprinkle with a little salt.

Meanwhile, in medium skillet cook zucchini pulp and tomato in butter till squash is tender, about 3 minutes. Add eggs, the ¼ teaspoon salt, and pepper. Cook over low heat till just set, lifting with spatula so uncooked portion runs underneath. Spoon egg mixture into zucchini shells. Top with cheese. Cover; heat till cheese melts. Makes 4 servings.

Stuffed Pattypan Squash

6 pattypan squash
4 slices bacon
⅓ cup finely chopped onion
¾ cup seasoned fine dry bread
  crumbs
½ cup milk

Cook whole squash in boiling salted water till just tender, 15 to 20 minutes. Drain; cool. Cut a small slice from stem end of each squash. Scoop out pulp, leaving ½-inch shell. Finely chop pulp; set aside. Sprinkle shells with salt. Cook bacon till crisp. Drain, reserving 2 tablespoons drippings. Crumble bacon; set aside. Cook onion in reserved drippings till tender. Stir in crumbs, milk, and squash pulp. Fill shells; top with bacon. Bake, covered, in 12x7½x2-inch baking dish at 350° for 30 to 35 minutes. Makes 6 servings.

Zucchini Nut Loaf

1 cup grated zucchini squash
1 cup sugar
1 egg
½ cup cooking oil
1½ cups all-purpose flour
1 teaspoon ground cinnamon
½ teaspoon baking soda
½ teaspoon ground nutmeg
¼ teaspoon baking powder
¼ teaspoon finely shredded lemon
  peel
½ cup chopped walnuts

In mixing bowl beat together zucchini, sugar, and egg. Add cooking oil; mix well. Stir together flour, cinnamon, baking soda, nutmeg, baking powder, lemon peel, and ½ teaspoon salt. Stir into zucchini mixture. Fold in walnuts. Pour into a greased 8½x4½x2½-inch loaf pan. Bake at 325° till done, 60 to 65 minutes. Cool in pan on rack for 10 minutes; remove from pan. Cool thoroughly on rack. Wrap and store overnight before slicing. Makes 1 loaf.

Zucchini Relish

4 to 4½ pounds zucchini squash
2 medium onions
1 sweet red pepper
2 tablespoons salt
2 cups sugar
1 cup vinegar
1 cup water
2 teaspoons celery seed
1 teaspoon ground turmeric
1 teaspoon ground nutmeg

Cut up vegetables; grind in food chopper, using coarse blade. Add salt. Cover; refrigerate overnight. Rinse in cold water. Drain well. In 4- to 5-quart kettle combine vegetable mixture, sugar, vinegar, water, celery seed, turmeric, nutmeg, and ⅛ teaspoon pepper. Bring to boil. Cover; boil gently for 10 minutes; stir often. Ladle hot mixture into hot, clean pint jars; leave ½-inch headspace. Prepare lids according to manufacturer's directions. Wipe jar rim. Adjust lid. Process jars in boiling water bath 15 minutes (start timing when water returns to boil). Makes 4 pints.

Vegetable Combinations

Old-Fashioned Fresh Vegetable-Beef Soup

  3 **pounds beef shank cross cuts**
  8 **cups water**
  4 **teaspoons salt**
  ½ **teaspoon dried oregano,
       crushed**
  ¼ **teaspoon dried marjoram,
       crushed**
  5 **whole black peppercorns**
  2 **bay leaves**
  4 **fresh ears of corn** *or* **1
       10-ounce package frozen
       whole kernel corn**
  3 **tomatoes, peeled and cut up**
  2 **medium potatoes, peeled and
       cubed (2 cups)**
  1 **cup fresh** *or* **½ of a 9-ounce
       package frozen cut green
       beans**
  2 **medium carrots, sliced (1 cup)**
  2 **ribs celery, sliced (1 cup)**
  1 **medium onion, chopped (½ cup)**

In large kettle or Dutch oven combine beef cross cuts, water, salt, oregano, marjoram, peppercorns, and bay leaves. Bring mixture to boiling. Reduce heat; cover and simmer for 2 hours. Remove the beef. Cut meat from bones; chop meat. Strain broth; skim off excess fat. Return broth to kettle. Cut fresh corn from cobs. Add the chopped meat, fresh or frozen corn, tomatoes, potatoes, green beans, carrots, celery, and onion. Simmer, covered, for 1 hour. Season to taste with salt and pepper. Makes 10 to 12 servings.

Garden Row Salad

3 medium carrots, sliced
1 large cucumber, cut up
1 pint cherry tomatoes, halved
4 ribs celery, sliced
1½ cups croutons
4 ounces sharp Cheddar cheese
½ slice bread, torn in pieces
2 hard-cooked eggs, sliced
6 slices bacon, crisp-cooked
Choice of salad dressing

Place carrots in blender; cover with *cold* water. Cover container; blend till coarsely chopped. Drain well. Place carrots in glass salad bowl. Discard cucumber seeds. Repeat above blending procedure for cucumber; drain and layer atop carrots. Place tomatoes atop cucumber. Repeat the blending procedure for celery; drain and layer atop tomatoes. Place croutons atop celery. Wipe blender dry. Cube cheese; place in blender with bread. Cover; blend till coarsely chopped. Layer with eggs atop salad. Crumble bacon; sprinkle atop. To serve, toss with dressing. Serves 10 to 12.

Succotash

2 cups fresh *or* 1 10-ounce package frozen baby lima beans
2 ounces salt pork (optional)
½ teaspoon sugar
4 fresh ears of corn *or* 1 10-ounce package frozen whole kernel corn
⅓ cup light cream
1 tablespoon all-purpose flour

In saucepan combine lima beans, salt pork, sugar, ½ cup water, ½ teaspoon salt, and dash pepper. Cover and simmer till limas are almost tender, about 20 minutes. Cut fresh corn from cobs. Stir fresh or frozen corn into lima mixture. Cover and simmer till vegetables are tender, about 12 minutes more. Remove salt pork. Slowly blend light cream into the flour; stir into vegetable mixture. Cook and stir till thickened and bubbly. Makes 6 servings.

Vegetable Tempura

Assorted fresh vegetables such as asparagus spears, green onion, cauliflower, sweet potatoes, mushrooms, green beans, and zucchini squash
Cooking oil for deep-fat frying
1 cup all-purpose flour
1 slightly beaten egg
2 tablespoons cooking oil
½ teaspoon sugar
Condiments

Wash and dry vegetables well. Slice or cut into strips or pieces, if desired. Using a skillet at least 3 inches deep, pour in cooking oil to depth of 1½ inches. Heat to 365°. For batter, combine flour, egg, the 2 tablespoons oil, sugar, 1 cup *ice* water, and ½ teaspoon salt. Beat just till moistened (a few lumps should remain). Stir in 1 or 2 ice cubes. *Use at once.* Dip vegetables into batter. Fry in hot oil, several at a time, till light brown; drain on paper toweling. Serve with *Condiments:* (1) grated gingerroot; (2) equal parts grated turnip and radish, mixed; (3) ½ cup prepared mustard mixed with 3 tablespoons soy sauce.

Louisiana Relish

10 fresh ears of corn
4 large onions
2 large green peppers, halved
2 sweet red peppers, halved
2 medium cucumbers
4 ribs celery
1 small head cabbage
2 small dried hot red peppers
1 clove garlic
2½ cups packed brown sugar
2 tablespoons all-purpose flour
3 cups vinegar

Cut corn from cobs; set aside. Using coarse blade of food grinder, grind onions, green and red peppers, cucumbers, celery, cabbage, hot peppers, and garlic. Combine ground vegetables with corn; stir in ¼ cup salt. Cover; chill overnight. Rinse and drain mixture. Combine brown sugar and flour; stir in vinegar and ½ cup water. Pour over vegetables. Bring mixture to boiling; boil gently 5 minutes. Ladle hot mixture into hot, clean pint jars; leave ½-inch headspace.

Prepare lids according to manufacturer's directions. Wipe off rim of jar. Adjust lid on jar. Process jars in boiling water bath for 15 minutes (start timing when water returns to boil). Makes 6 pints relish.

Index